Using
Puppetry
in the
Church

Using Puppetry in the Church

Edited by

Everett Robertson

BROADMAN PRESS
Nashville, Tennessee

Dewey Decimal classification number: 791.5
Subject Heading: PUPPETS AND PUPPET PLAYS
Printed in the United States of America

Contributors:

Joe and Gloria Morrell: Professional Puppeteers. Currently Joe is Minister of Music, First Baptist Church, Bradenton, Florida. Contributed ideas relating to producing with puppets.

Lyn Yarborough: Founded Puppets 'n' Stuff performing company. Primary writer of *The Puppet Ministry Handbook*. Currently she is Art Director, Public Relations Department, Baptist General Convention of Texas. Contributed to Chapters 3 and 6.

Everett Robertson: Drama Specialist, Church Recreation Department, Church Services and Materials Division, Baptist Sunday School Board. Compiled and edited.

Pattern Contributors:

Sarah Walton Miller, Dramatist and Puppeteer, Houston, Texas.
Joan King, Teacher and Puppeteer, Jasper, Alabama.
Carroll Brown, Puppeteer and Foreign Missionary to Africa.
Doris Goodrich Jones, Puppeteer, Waco, Texas.
Kaywin LaNoue, Teacher and Puppeteer, Nashville, Tennessee.
Joy Robertson, Dramatist and Puppeteer, Nashville, Tennessee.

Contents

Introduction

This book is intended to provide basic techniques and materials to develop a puppet ministry. Essentially it is a beginning handbook, although there are techniques many ongoing puppet ministries will find valuable. The book can be read from start to finish, but it was designed with the idea that the reader will use various sections as they are needed.

The book provides not only techniques to develop puppet ministry teams but also information to be used by any individual or church organization desiring to use puppets as a communication tool. Children, youth, and adult workers will find material to enable them to use puppets at any level with their age-groups. Music personnel will discover methods to help teach and perform music with all ages. Recreation directors, youth directors, and others planning socials, fellowships, banquets, and retreats will find the manual useful.

The book should be an excellent resource for church libraries. The large and varied number of puppet patterns make it a good resource for day camping, Vacation Bible School, and crafts programs. In fact, wherever puppets can help communicate, this book will be valuable.

Many of the patterns in the book have been reduced to conserve space. These may be enlarged in several ways. One approach is to simply sketch them in freehand at the necessary size. Another method is to use an overhead projector to enlarge them to the necessary dimensions. Butcher paper is cheap and adequate for this purpose.

The book contains only short demonstration scripts for Bible teaching. Another book, *Puppet Scripts for Use at Church*, supports this product. The script collection includes scripts for promotion, Bible study and worship, special seasons, general use, and fun and fellowship. Selected scripts are produced on a one-hour cassette tape that accompanies the collection. Scripts in the collection are varied in form and style as well as length.

Because of the wide variety of patterns and other material, beginning puppeteers should not be discouraged by advanced material. Rather, select that material which is appropriate for the beginning ministry. More involved and advanced techniques in the book may or may not be used at a later date.

Puppetry is an art form. Therefore, this book does not pretend to be a comprehensive study of puppetry in the church. Rather, it presents guidelines through which the church puppeteer can creatively develop and mold his own form and style. No two puppet ministries will ever be alike if each strives to fit the specific needs of its church. When this premise is followed, puppetry will be an invaluable communication tool for every church.

Chapter 1
A COMMUNICATION TOOL

A Philosophy

Communication of the message of Jesus Christ to the world is the primary concern for all Christians. Methods of communication change as the world changes. Twentieth century Christians have a responsibility to discover and develop new methods of communication. History has proven puppetry a viable means of communication. From earliest man to the Middle Ages to the twentieth century, puppetry has successfully interpreted human characteristics. The raging popularity of cartoon figures and Sesame Street characters demonstrates the validity of puppetry as a communication medium today. Churches everywhere are discovering the value of puppets in their ministry.

A puppet is any inanimate object that takes on human characteristics when manipulated by humans. A puppet can be a spoon with a painted face, or a large, elegantly-designed figure. There is no limit to the subject matter available for expression with puppets. They can say things in a way impossible through other communication mediums.

The great versatility of the puppet makes it an excellent communicative tool for the church. A puppet may entertain, promote, announce, teach, and train almost in the same breath. Puppets are loved by children, but their value in the church extends far beyond children's work. Youth are often the core of a puppet ministry with their imagination and creativity. Adults are fascinated and interested in the magic of a puppet. Senior adults can be important components in the puppet ministry by serving as puppeteers or by constructing puppets.

The magical power of a puppet is an excellent method to support all aspects of the church program. A leading quality of puppets is their ability to cross age barriers. Children, youth, and adults can be simultaneously communicated with through puppetry. Social and racial barriers can also be crossed by puppets, making them particularly suitable to programs of outreach. A puppet's ability to immediately command attention permits it to point-blank fire the message of Jesus Christ to the lost—many of whom close their senses to other means of communication.

Puppets are unreal entities, and because of this extreme care must be taken when they are used in the church. A primary reason for their powerful ability to communicate is that an audience will listen because they know the puppets are not "real." It is important that children understand puppets are not real beings. Otherwise, the child may place more faith in the puppet than in the message the puppet is delivering. When the child fully comprehends what a puppet is and its role, then the puppet becomes a wonderful teaching tool.

A puppet acts out or represents human situations in much the same way an actor does. An actor portrays a character, but the actor can never literally become that character. The same is true of a puppet. A puppet may represent the actions of a character only so long as he is portraying the character. For example, a puppet might pray while portraying Peter in a Bible story, but a puppet cannot lead in a prayer session. To use a puppet as a worship or prayer leader would be a grave misrepresentation of those activities. They are real; a puppet is not.

A puppet is simply a megaphone for the Christian similar to literature, radio, and television. These mediums are only communicative tools, hardly ends in themselves. A puppet is primarily a unique device to better communicate the ongoing church program and ministry.

Puppets at Work

Puppets can serve in some capacity in most areas of the ministry of the church. There are certain types of material that puppets handle very well. Puppets can attract attention, make announcements, promote programs or activities, entertain, teach, and train. The techniques involved in these areas can be applied to other types of material a puppet may be called on to communicate.

Attract attention—The color, hyperactive spirit, and overall fascinating qualities give puppets the ability to immediately attract attention. How long that attention is sustained depends on the audience, subject matter, adeptness of the puppeteers, and other factors. Puppets can introduce programs or speakers in Sunday School, Church Training, and other programs. They can introduce characters or situations for emphasis in Bible Study. They can present basic arguments to be probed in Church Training. Puppets are excellent tools for outreach. They can attract new members to the bus ministry. They can perform in a shopping center and in a few seconds draw attention to the church and its program and total ministry.

Announcements—The puppet's ability to attract attention makes it a natural medium through which to make announcements. Puppets have been used successfully in worship services on Sunday morning, evening, and Wednesday evening to announce church activities. In fact, anywhere announcements are needed the puppet is a viable tool for making them. Formats can vary, but a simple one is to have one puppet ignorant of the announced activity. One puppet must repeat the information several times until the other finally understands.

Promotion—The puppet's unique ability to plunge to the basis of a situation without offending groups or individuals makes it an excellent tool for promotion. Stewardship in particular is an area in which puppets can probe in their innocent, childlike manner. Puppets are particularly effective when they leap to extremes. One puppet gives everything; the other puppet may give nothing. They argue their philosophies, neither of which is real, and then compromise. The compromise may be based on the facts regarding stewardship that are expressed in the argument. Again, it is crucial that the puppet show be short and to the point.

Entertainment—To a certain extent, puppets always entertain. As a result, they are a natural and lively addition to banquets, fellowships, and socials. They can tell jokes, pantomime music, and generally fit pleasantly into any atmosphere where people want to relax and have fun. Puppets can emcee banquets or variety shows, or work with a master of ceremonies. Puppets can represent the church at school and community activities. They can perform for clubs and other civic organizations. They can appear on local television shows, or on their own show at a cable television station. This ability permits them to entertain and at the same time be a vibrant means of outreach.

Teaching—One of the best ways puppets can serve the church is as teaching aides. They are particularly successful with children. They may be the key to teaching youth and adults when other communication techniques with those groups appear to break down. Puppets can tell Bible stories or modern parables in many formats. They can teach Bible verses to children. They can teach songs and basic musical techniques to children. With youth and adults they can state—and restate—various types of information. They can review material that has been taught. Their review will of course be from a puppet's point of view, which can be entertaining as well as enlightening.

Training—Any training material that can be presented verbally can be communicated by puppets. Certain types of nonverbal techniques can also be presented through puppets. They can introduce a training session by portraying how something should not be done. The session corrects their errors. They can appear periodically through the session and get the procedures all mixed up. The audience or leader corrects them and in doing so reviews the material.

Working Formats

Puppets can work in many different formats to achieve the desired goal. A puppet and a person has been a popular combination for many years. Successful teams include Howdy Doody and Buffalo Bob, Lamb Chop and Shari Lewis, Mr. Moose and Captain Kangaroo, and many others. In this format the audience identifies immediately with the person, who in turn acts as a liason between the puppet and the audience.

A singular puppet can perform very short monologues. Two or more puppets can work in ensemble to tell a story. Or, they can combine with actors (people) to present a play. Puppets can be used with children or youth choirs in musicals. For example, in *Jonah's Tale of a Whale,* (Broadman Press) the puppets can portray the dramatic parts while the choir sings. The same is true of *David's Hotshot Slingshot* (Broadman Press) and *It's Cool in the Furnace* (Word).

Puppet productions may be carefully prepared, or totally improvisational. The way puppets are used depends directly on the occasion, audience, and the experience of the puppeteers. Prepared productions may be taped or live. These are particularly suitable for more formal occasions and large groups. However, if a prepared production is pre-taped, a certain amount of spontaneity will be lost in performance.

Improvisational performances are excellent in teaching and performing for smaller groups. This technique permits total spontaneity between audience and puppet. It also requires experienced and quick-thinking puppeteers. To maintain a high audience response level in such a performance, the puppeteer must be able to totally handle the puppet, physically and mentally.

Chapter 2
THE PUPPET MINISTRY

Establishing a Puppet Ministry

Establishing a puppet ministry in the church is one method of achieving high-quality puppetry productions that enhance the value of the puppet as a communicative tool.

The puppet ministry functions in the organizational structure of the church under the recreation ministry. Long-range planning, budgeting, and personnel are approved by the church council through the recreation staff (or committee). A puppet ministry director is appointed and he in turn recruits and assigns puppet teams.

A prime requirement for the puppet ministry director is enthusiasm for the potential of puppetry in the church. Experience helps, but it is not required. Interest, study, and hard work along with basic leadership ability can be the ingredients for a wide-ranging and meaningful puppet ministry.

The director establishes an organizational structure for his particular puppet ministry based on resources, both human and financial. The director determines budget needs and plans and coordinates all aspects of the ministry. He selects puppeteers as well as other personnel for the construction of puppets, development of scenery, props, lighting, and costumes, and any other special personnel required.

The director actively pursues performance possibilities. This may include contacting all Sunday School and Church Training leaders, and working with the church staff and organizational personnel. Then he plans and initiates any special action necessary to prepare the puppet team or the production area for the performance. After the performance the director carefully documents it in a notebook which is used to record all performances.

The notebook includes the name of the organization for which the production was performed and the occasion. It should also include the date, length of the production, and titles of one or more works used in the performances. It is helpful to document who the puppeteers were, and to keep a copy of the program and specific scripts or scenarios used (see illustration of the sample page).

Maintaining proper records will preclude the repetition of script materials with the same group. Also, it is helpful to make a notation regarding the acceptance of the material by the audience. This procedure will aid in planning future events with the same audience.

A major function of the director is to carefully select personnel, then plan and activate rehearsals to prepare the personnel. Puppet teams may vary in number, but a good working number is four members per team. This figure may change, depending on the amount of space behind stage and the number of characters. Of course, there is no limit to the age or number of people who can participate in a puppet ministry. A church may have many teams, and other organizations in the church may assist the puppet ministry at various times. For example, senior adults may construct costumes and/or props. Adults may build stages, special lighting, scenery, and props. (See organizational chart)

Generally, children are not included in puppet teams. This does not prevent children from occasionally presenting their own puppet shows in Vacation Bible School, for example. But, a child's value is limited in an ongoing puppet ministry. The primary group who will readily participate in the ministry are youth. How devoted youth are to the puppet ministry will depend to some extent on how successful they are and how their peers judge their success. Young adults are another group from which to draw personnel. Some churches have working adult teams and senior adult teams. The extent of participation by the latter two groups will depend on the size of the church and the amount of interest and excitement stimulated by the puppet ministry director.

It is crucial that the director plan adequate rehearsals to train puppeteers. Periodic training sessions should be planned to enlist and train new personnel as well as to replace team members who have resigned. This is the only way the puppet ministry can be maintained and developed over a period of years.

Inexperienced puppeteers are easily discouraged if they perform badly through lack of preparation. Children are quick to see flaws in productions. They may openly comment, "His mouth isn't moving with his words!" or "How can he do that, he isn't looking at the other puppet?" Youth and adult audiences will be quickly bored and even embarrassed when puppeteers are inept.

Achieving control of a puppet to the point the puppeteer is free to express himself through the

Notebook Sample Page

Audience Group:

Contact Person:

Place of Performance:

Occasion:

Date:

Length of Program:

Program Material (skits, songs, etc.):

Puppets Used:

Props Used:

Names of Puppeteers:

puppet is an exciting and rewarding experience. Many people who have difficulty expressing themselves in other communication mediums may be natural puppeteers. Handling puppets can also be a method of opening up introverted youth or adults.

The director should encourage competition between teams; and in the assigning of each team he should keep them as even as possible. Teams should be encouraged to work together and seek new ways of communicating with their puppets. Over a period of time, teams will become adept at improvising with puppets. As the teams gain experience and confidence, the length of their scripts may be increased. It is important, however, that early efforts be short and episodic.

Special personnel whom the director must select include: A scenery and properties coordinator, a sound consultant, a lighting director, and someone to store and maintain the puppets and other equipment. The consultant for purchasing and maintaining sound equipment can teach the puppeteers to handle the equipment. Later he will only be needed at regular intervals to check out the equipment. If sound and lighting equipment are run from in front of the puppet stage, a special person will be needed to work each production. Unless there are numerous sound and light cues, the puppeteers can normally work the equipment from backstage. Sound and light levels can be more accurate for each performance, however, if they are run from behind or near the audience. (See technical personnel chart)

Rehearsals

Rehearsals are an essential item to the puppetry ministry; they should be planned well in advance. Ideally, weekly rehearsals can be scheduled in the existing church calendar. If this schedule is impossible, or impractical, a rehearsal week should be selected every six to eight weeks. Four, five or more rehearsals should be scheduled during that week, and the director must rigorously enforce the schedule. The best procedure, however, is to plan one rehearsal per week.

The length of a rehearsal may vary, but avoid a rehearsal extending longer than two hours. An hour should be sufficient to prepare a three- or four-minute puppet production. To save time, different teams may rehearse together. The teams can take turns criticizing each others' efforts. Also, by watching each other, team members will grow together and many preliminary errors can be avoided.

Beginning rehearsals should be spent on learning to manipulate the puppets. Then, each puppet character will need a voice. The puppeteer should play with his puppet and talk back and forth with it to develop the character. Next, the characters rehearse together to interpret the script. The director must assist in interpretation, staging, and basic communication with the audience.

Prior to rehearsal the director spends the necessary time to prepare. This includes careful examination of the script. In this examination the director should ask several questions: What is the intent of the script? How is this intent expressed? What is the basic conflict in the situation? How do the characters act and react to the conflict? How is each character different? What does each character do and in general contribute to the script? What scenery, props, lights, and sound are necessary? These basic questions must be answered by the director. The director must also be sensitive to rhythm, builds, and climaxes in the script. In short puppet scripts the director can answer these questions almost instantly on careful reading and study. With longer puppet productions it will not be as easy.

If time to prepare a script and adequately rehearse is limited, the production must be short. The longer the work, the more rehearsal time required to prepare it for performance. Every attempt must be made to keep early productions short until the puppeteers have complete control of their work.

An idea to enliven early rehearsals is to bring a bicycle horn or something similar to rehearsal. Tell a member of the observing team to honk the horn everytime the rehearsing team does something wrong (poor posture, poor mouth movement, inconsistent eye contact, improper entrances and exits). Reverse the procedure when the other team observes. It is amazing how quickly both teams will improve their techniques. This process encourages the puppeteers to be aware of bad techniques and correct them immediately. The fewer honks there are during a rehearsal, the closer the team is to being ready to perform that particular skit.

Arrange a checkout system so that the puppeteers can take scripts or tapes home during the week to work on and memorize. Personal rehearsal time by each puppeteer will minimize the amount of time spent together.

Manipulating Hand Puppets

A few basic techniques must be mastered before a puppet will become an efficient communicator. However, because puppetry is an art form, the fine points and subtlety of manipulation will be up to the individual puppeteer. Experience and determi-

Organization Chart

	Name	Address	Phone Number
Director:			
Asst. Director:			
Team I:			
Team II:			
Team III:			
Tour Planning Director:			
Promotion Director:			

Technical Personnel

	Name	Address	Phone Number
Puppet Construction Assistants:			
Costume Assistants:			
Sound Assistants:			
Lighting Assistants:			
Scenery Assistants:			
Properties Assistants:			
Maintenance Assistants:			

Sample Rehearsal Schedule

Date	Time	Puppeteers Called	Place	Scene to be Rehearsed

nation by the puppeteer to make the puppet increasingly lifelike will be primary factors in how far the puppeteer's artistry develops.

The puppeteer should watch as many puppet shows as possible. This includes televised as well as live performances. Also, observation of cartoons either filmed or printed will be helpful. It is important that the puppeteer gain an understanding and feeling for what a puppet does and how he does it. For example, puppets tend to be quick and hyperactive. But, sometimes this must be suggested through the feeling of the puppeteer. Simply jerking the puppet around quickly is not enough.

An understanding of timing is also important. Sometimes this is a natural talent, but it can also be achieved through observation and experience. By constantly observing puppets and cartoon figures, the puppeteer will gradually begin to understand how and why puppets do what they do successfully. When the puppeteer begins to control these unstated characteristics of puppets, his craftsmanship will greatly improve and become an item to take pride in.

"Lip sync" is a term to describe the coordination of the mouth action of the puppet with the spoken words. Accurate lip sync greatly improves communication. A natural appearance is most desirable; however, trying to make a mouth movement for every syllable of every word is not always natural for a puppet. This constant movement will result in a bobbing up and down of the puppet's head. Simply try to capture the rhythm of the words. A puppet should not have the appearance of biting his words. Rather, he should have a more natural openness to his mouth action. The mouth should be completely closed between syllables and between words.

Focus on vowel sounds to begin. Control of the vowel sounds is of primary importance. Consonants are quick and often may be avoided entirely. The beginning puppeteer may wish to rehearse without the puppet. As he speaks, he opens and closes his hand until the hand begins to express the word being stated. If the puppeteer can mentally coordinate the process of opening his mouth with the process of opening his hand, he will quickly achieve efficiency of lip sync.

Actors learn that the most important part of their physique is their eyes. The same is true of the puppet. The direction of the eyes will determine the focus of the audience. When two puppets speak with each other, they should also look at one another, not off to the side or above the head of the other puppet. The same is true when a puppet talks or sings to an audience. Practice until the puppeteer has the right feel about the position of his hand in regard to audience eye contact. Compensate upward or downward if the audience is standing or sitting.

Entering and exiting with puppets requires special techniques. Unless it is for a special effect, a puppet should never just pop up; instead, it should walk on and walk off. This is done by having the puppet gradually appear from a side wing or the rear of the stage. By using a slight up and down movement of his arm, the puppeteer will give the effect that the puppet is walking. If the puppet needs to run, simply speed everything up. Once the puppet is in view, it should stand erect, not slouching or leaning on the stage. Generally, all puppets should be of uniform height.

Each character has its own style and rhythm of movement. The age, energy, and general attitude of the character will directly affect this style and rhythm.

If a puppet is not speaking, he is listening; and listening is as important to the total production as speaking. Puppets should agree or disagree with what is being said. Small vocal reactions are possible, as long as they do not distract from the speaker. If the director is not familiar with basic staging techniques, the best procedure is to simply watch and let the eye judge. If something doesn't look quite right, make changes until it does. With time and experience the director can logically determine how to time entrances, exits, and movements on the stage.

Final rehearsals should be conducted similarly to performances. It is the director's responsibility to ensure that the production runs smoothly in performance. He must be certain that the puppet characters are consistent and that they communicate the important information. He must coordinate lights, scenery, props, and any special effects with the action of the script. Nothing should be left to chance in performance. One slight error in lighting, sound, or whatever can spoil what might otherwise be an exciting performance.

Remember that audiences can be not only understanding but also highly critical—particularly children. Lack of proper rehearsal will be easily recognized and will directly affect that performance. Over a period of time insufficient, or inefficient rehearsal can destroy the positive values of a puppet ministry.

Working Space

Several options are available in determining the necessary space for a developing puppet ministry. An advantage in using puppets as a communication tool is that they are very flexible. They can be used in permanent surroundings or in a compact, portable capacity. Ideally, the puppet ministry will have sufficient space and equipment to work in either of those capacities.

If a relatively large, permanent room is available in the church, the ministry will have adequate storage space and a place to grow. In this room a permanent or semipermanent puppet stage can be constructed. Various groups will come to that room for special performances. The advantages of this type of operation are many. Rehearsal space is always available, and the basic equipment, stage, and so forth are already set up. Puppets and technical equipment can be stored near the spot they will be used in performances. Thus, equipment and other physical items used by the puppet team won't be scattered around the church. Storage can be a real problem if several different performances are given on a Sunday morning in Sunday School. Also, in a permanent room, various tools and maintenance items are close at hand for construction of new puppets, props, and scenery.

Often, however, the ministry will have to share space with other church programs and activities. If this is the case, it is essential that special storage space be provided for a stage or stages, sound equipment, lighting equipment, scenery, props, costumes, puppets, and any other equipment or supplies used in the ministry. Because puppets and puppet stages are often composed primarily of fabric materials, they can quickly deteriorate if not properly stored and maintained. Lack of adequate storage space could double or triple the cost of maintaining the puppet ministry over a year.

Whether the working space is permanent or temporary, the ministry will need sufficient room for rehearsals, construction of props, scenery, and puppets, and maintenance of lighting and sound equipment.

The storage space may be a closet with shelves or cabinets that can be locked. The space available should be divided into areas: puppets, lights, sound, props, scenery, tools, etc. Puppets, for example, should be stored in plastic bags and placed on shelves. If these are not available, take an old hat rack and hang string from it with clothes pins attached at the end. The puppets can be hooked onto the clothes hangers, and the entire rack can be covered with cellophane or plastic. It is important that the storage space be relatively dry and clean. If dust or dirt is allowed to gather, the bright colors of the puppets and their scenery can soon become dull.

Even if a permanent home is available, there should be some equipment set aside for touring. This equipment should be as light as possible and stored in sturdy trunks or crates that can be handled easily.

Some general maintenance items should be kept handy. Scotchguard or a similar product is necessary to spray the puppets for protection of their appearance. Other items are: scissors, glue, velcro strips, pipe cleaners, boxes of pins, rubber bands, duct tape (for taping down electrical wires), and brushes for grooming the puppets.

Writing the Puppet Script

Developing script materials is a necessity for any ongoing puppet ministry. Occasionally an individual in the church may be willing to spend the time required to write good, sound scripts. However, more often than not the scripts will be developed by the director and puppeteers.

The best method of assembling a script is to begin with a scenario. A "scenario" is an outline for a play or some other form of dramatic action. The puppet team selects major points to be displayed through the action of the puppets and outlines those points. Then the puppeteers improvise with the puppets until the design of the script begins to take shape. With experience this will be a quick process.

In the process of assembling the script the team considers several steps. First, determine the intent of the script. Second, select a situation that can be the sounding board for the intent of the script. The situation may be real or imaginary, but it must permit the characters to fully explore the questions involved in the script's intent. Third, select characters that naturally fit into the situation. If the team has one or more characters that appear regularly in its performances, the script may be built around them. To have action in the script, there must be some type of conflict. The conflict may exist between two or more characters, between the character and an external force, or in the character himself. Outline the action that results from the conflict and how the conflict is finally resolved.

Fourth, determine how the characters act and react to the conflict and the situation in which they are involved. Outline the main action the puppets pursue. For longer works, small actions will feed into the large, continuing action. Fifth, give the characters specific dialogue that expresses their opinions regarding their present situation.

To further enhance puppet scripts, observe the following general rules. In very short scripts (one to two minutes) be precise and to the point. Do not dally with a lot of character development, establishing the situation, or unessential dialogue —particularly jokes. In longer works break the actions into short scenes. Remember to always include introductory action and a satisfying conclusion. Be careful not to leave any questions unanswered unless for a specific purpose. Be creative with situation, character, and dialogue. Avoid hackneyed or cliché phrases.

Be sure to keep in mind some basic things about puppets. They are quick, fantastical characters. They speak in short, jumpy phrases. They may jump to illogical conclusions as quickly as they do logical ones. Also, they have a tendency to leap to extremes in character and situation. Their pace is always quick, light, and bouncy. These feelings should be suggested in script materials, not only in physical representations.

Touring with Puppets

Unlimited opportunities exist for short as well as extended tours with puppets. The primary ingredients for a successful tour include an experienced puppet team, equipment for touring, and a comfortable tour schedule.

The following is a list of potential areas, both local and otherwise, to tour with puppet productions: local schools, civic clubs and local organizations, parks in the summer, other churches, other Vacation Bible Schools, to mission areas, local hospitals and retirement homes, shopping malls, local fairs and other events where large numbers of people may be gathered. Puppets can also be used with tours of other church organizations, particularly the choir. Basically, puppets can tour anywhere there are people who will see them and who will accept their performances.

Completely portable equipment is a necessity. Otherwise, heavy stages, lights, and sound equipment will take considerable time to assemble before a performance, and to remove afterwards. Sound equipment must be sufficient, portable, and preferably designed for touring. Lighting can be minimal. The amount of portable lighting will depend on the group, transportation space, and the requirements of the productions. Stages must be light, yet durable. Plastic pipe stages with curtains are recommended.

Puppets, props, and all equipment must be stored in crates or trunks. These should be sufficiently padded and waterproofed if possible. Cardboard boxes and similar containers should be avoided. Puppets should be stored in cellophane bags before being packed. Every effort should be made to keep them from coming into contact with dirty surfaces or being crushed from too tight packing. If the puppet team or teams plans regular touring, it is recommended that specific crates be constructed for all

of the equipment. These should be light but durable. The interior of the crate should be designed so that every part of touring equipment has a place. This lengthens the life of the equipment and precludes anything being left at a performance location. Inexpensive trunks in local budget stores are alternatives to crates.

Planning an extended tour is not an easy proposition. Poor planning can prove to be a nightmare as the tour proceeds. Use a tour planning sheet to insure performance dates are scheduled with sufficient travel and rest time. Generally, a cushion should be allowed where possible in case of emergencies.

To schedule dates, allow contacts a number of dates and times to choose from. Plan to be in a certain area during a certain period of time. Backtracking may be necessary to meet performance requests. If the tour must partially support itself financially, negotiate a contract with each contact. If you are touring churches, request that they provide a meal or lodging. An extended tour can be a costly venture. Budget carefully to cover the complete cost of the tour. Then add an additional ten to fifteen percent to cover rising prices and emergencies.

Inform the contact well in advance of any special needs at the performance site such as equipment, lights, sound, space, or whatever. Determine the minimal amount of space necessary to set up all equipment and run the performance. Then determine the ideal amount of space. Send both figures to all contacts. Make arrangements with the contact person to provide personnel to set up equipment or otherwise assist with the performance. Touring costs can be cut considerably by using local personnel at each performance site for nonperformance duties.

Before the tour begins have a complete record of correspondence with contacts in hand. The tour director should keep a list of all contact phone numbers and addresses with him at all times during the tour. Also, it is advisable to have the phone numbers as well addresses of motels and restaurants where reservations have been made. Also keep a list of emergency phone numbers in major areas being toured.

Make certain church insurance covers all phases of the tour. If it doesn't, purchase a special travel policy that will cover all personnel and equipment for the duration of the tour.

Above all, keep the atmosphere as relaxed as possible on extended tours. Permit puppeteers plenty of time to relax and enjoy the tour. A tight performance and travel schedule leads to a tight and tense atmosphere among the touring group.

An annual puppet ministry tour can be a meaning-

Puppet Ministry Tour Planning Sheet

Date	Performance Time	Place (Address)	Contact Person	Phone Number	Travel Time	Lodging

ful and rewarding experience. It can serve to build spirit on the puppet team. Also, it permits the team a special goal to work for by improving their production technique. Finally, it can help spread the puppet ministry to areas and churches that previously were ignorant of its value as a communication tool.

Chapter 3
A TEACHING TOOL

Teaching with Puppets

Every teacher should consider the use of puppets as a solution to communication problems. It should be noted, however, that puppets are only tools, not an automatic solution to every problem. Except for short-term programs, such as Vacation Bible School or Day Camping, puppets generally should not be used every session. However, when used properly, they can be most effective in getting attention and communicating a message. Here are four ways puppets can be used to teach:

Introduce a new unit—This approach gives special emphasis and a clearer understanding of objectives at the beginning of a new period of study.

Repetitive events and welcoming class members at the beginning of each session—This approach should be done at the same time and with the same puppet so the group anticipates its arrival and becomes familiar with its personality.

Bible story recall—In teaching Bible stories it is often preferable to tell the Bible story in the traditional manner—holding the Bible open to the passage and telling the story in your own words, while maintaining eye contact with the group. There are several reasons for not substituting a puppet show for the telling of Bible stories. As a teacher, you may not have the proper puppets for Bible stories—especially a different one each week. Many Bible stories are difficult to act out without elaborate props, costumes, and many puppets; these provisions are not practical for a one-time story. One other reason to tell the story with the Bible in hand is to be sure that the students understand that the story you are telling is not just another entertaining story, but a true-to-life story from the Bible, God's Word. This is especially important if they have a weak background in Bible study. However, as we will see in later examples, puppets are extremely effective in helping to reinforce the facts and meaning of the story.

Memory verse exercises—Puppets can be used more effectively for teaching Bible verses than for almost anything else. Students will eagerly repeat the Bible verse and discuss its meaning through puppets.

Format for Teaching

Puppets can be used in many different ways to assist in the areas discussed earlier. Here are some suggested formats:

With a script—Sometimes a written script is the only way to make all the points that need to be made. You can create characters, establish settings, and plan the action and dialogue for maximum impact. The script may be memorized, recorded, or roughly learned with a script pinned inside the stage to glance at from time to time. Keep the language simple and the story uncluttered; use as much action as possible.

Ad lib—In the classroom, spontaneous dialogue with the audience is probably the most common technique. It offers the most flexibility, allowing the greatest participation by the group. Participation by the group is very important; and it is this feature that distinguishes between puppetry as an inspirational, entertaining medium and puppetry as a teaching aide.

With or without a stage—For classroom purposes, a puppet stage is a minor concern. It is helpful to have one from time to time, but it need not be elaborate. Its primary requirements are ease of construction and erection, and a size small enough to keep from using up too much valuable floor space. Sometimes a stage isn't needed at all. This is especially true among preschoolers. These young children completely accept a puppet on the end of your arm in spite of the fact that your mouth moves along with the puppet's mouth.

If a stage is not used, a special purpose "puppet home" might be considered. This stage could be a large potato chip container with an opening in the side to reach into and pop the puppet up through an opening in the top. This stage would be good for the repetitive character who reminds children of tomorrow's or next week's activities, tells of refreshment time, challenges the children to invite a friend, or greets them at the beginning of the session. Maybe the puppet "sleeps" a lot, and the children awaken him by whistling or snapping their fingers. The teacher's imagination is the only limit to the number of variations on this idea.

The Classroom Puppeteer

The puppeteer in teaching may be the teacher or a special team. If it is the teacher, he or she must be willing to wear two hats. Hopefully the teacher's enthusiasm and excitement in his task will overcome any reluctance to be a puppeteer. There may be a tendency to be self-conscious in front of other teachers by affecting a comic voice and acting a little silly behind a curtain. There is a certain amount of dignity lost, to be sure, but perhaps much more will be gained. Actually, it's a lot of fun; and unless the teacher enters into the role enthusiastically, he will probably have to step aside and let others reap the benefits of using puppets.

The puppet team may also be used in classroom situations. The teacher should try to avoid using them as a "crutch" because they may be unavailable everytime he needs them. Also, the team will not be as familiar with the children as the teacher, and this fact will affect their efficiency in communication through puppets. The puppet team can be used effectively for banquet entertainment, seasonal emphases, unit introduction, and other similar areas.

A service project for the puppet team might be to develop puppet routines similar to those included at the end of this chapter, designed around themes common to children's literature. These routines, along with a set of puppets, could be kept in the library and checked out by the various organizations when needed. The teacher could, in turn, provide guidelines to the puppet team concerning good teaching techniques and age-level characteristics, as well as current copies of literature to use as source material.

Presenting the Story

Any story can be presented in many ways. The teacher should select the one that fits his circumstances. Major factors to be considered are: time, number and type of puppets, number and gender of the puppeteers (most Bible stories require male voices), and the age of the audience. Here are some possibilities for the presentation of the story of Zacchaeus and his encounter with Jesus at the Sycamore tree.

Traditional—The story can be acted out with a minimum of puppets, a tree, and a crowd prop (a cardboard cutout in the shape of a row of heads and shoulders, covered with cloth to look like the backs of people's heads).

Zacchaeus enters from behind the crowd, tries to see over their heads, attempts to break through, then mutters to himself about how they won't let him through. A voice from the crowd tells Zacchaeus, "Go away, Jesus won't want to see the likes of you!" Zacchaeus talks to himself about Jesus, and how he has heard that Jesus loves everyone, even tax collectors like himself.

Zacchaeus discovers the tree, climbs into it, and waits for Jesus to come by. Jesus enters from in front of the crowd, partially hidden from the audience, and announces to Zacchaeus that he must come down and take him, Jesus, home with him. With that, Zacchaeus comes down and they exit. The teacher can then tell what happened after that or change sets and act it out.

This is the traditional story. However, if the teacher lacks an adequate stage, props, puppets and male voices, he is not prevented from effectively telling this or any other story.

Interviewer and Zacchaeus—This method requires one puppet and an interviewer outside the stage. A stage, props, and additional puppets are not necessary. One word of caution. Be sure the interviewer involves the audience and keeps questions and answers short. Long monologues are boring. Concentrate on the main points, use some humor, and don't belabor the point or preach at the end. Perhaps let the children take turns asking Zacchaeus questions. The teacher can let older children take turns being Zacchaeus and operating the puppet while he, the teacher, asks them questions.

Different point of view—Many stories can be told by third parties or persons not directly mentioned in the biblical record. For example, how did people react to Zacchaeus when he began to give out his money? Zacchaeus, holding a bag in his hand, enters and approaches another puppet. The dialogue might be something like this:

ZACCHAEUS: Say, Benjamin, let me . . .

BENJAMIN: Go away, Zacchaeus, I paid my taxes last week.

ZACCHAEUS: I know, but . . .

BENJAMIN: And besides that, I paid twice last year. You tricked me!

ZACCHAEUS: Yes, but I want to give you all that back.

BENJAMIN: Oh, sure, sure you do, Zacchaeus.

ZACCHAEUS: I really do, Benjamin. Let me tell you what's happened to me.

Zacchaeus then tells the man about his meeting with Jesus, how he climbed the tree, and how his life has changed since he met Jesus. Again, keep the dialogue lively, not just a lengthy monologue by Zaccheaus.

Nonbiblical characters—There are many ways of using nonbiblical characters. One possibility for the Zacchaeus story might be to have a funny little character come along and discover an open Bible. The character begins reading under his breath and then reads a few key phrases of the Zacchaeus story. He begins to ask questions of another puppet, the teacher, or the children. The story is told through the process of reading, asking questions, and discussing answers.

Teaching Bible Verses

Puppets are very effective in teaching Bible verses to children. The following material covers several ways Bible verses can be taught with puppets. The methods the teacher selects are limited only by his imagination and creativity.

Children love to use puppets. An excellent method of teaching a Bible verse is to let the children play with the puppet and learn a verse at the same time. Teach the verse to the whole group with a puppet. Say it in unison once or twice. Then let the children come to the front, two or three at a time, and use the puppet(s) to lead the group in the verse. Amazingly, they will repeat the verse many times in order to have their turn.

Another method of teaching a Bible verse is to prepare a series of cards with a word of the verse on each card. During the script the cards are flipped over one at a time to face the audience. At a certain point in the verse other words are inserted. For example, "God loved us and sent (trees, rain, his son)."

JANEY: Hi, boys and girls, my name is Janey. This is my friend Joey. (*Improvise with the audience, discussing activities they have been involved in.*)

JOEY: Yeah, and we're going to talk about a Bible verse—uh—what's the the Bible verse, Janey?

JANEY: Okay, Joey, here's how it starts (*flips over first card "God"*). That's the first word, God.

JOEY: Oh, I know that word. That says "God."

JANEY: That's just the first word. Here's another one (*flips next card "loved"*).

JOEY: "God loved." We can say that much, can't we boys and girls? "God loved."

JANEY: (*flips next card "us"*). There it is. What does that say?

JOEY: "God loved us." That makes sense. We know about that, don't we boys and girls? Let's say that

together. "God loved us." That's a good verse. I like that. "God loved us."

JANEY: But that's not all the verse. There's more.

JOEY: There's more? What is it?

JANEY: (*flips next card "and sent"*). Here it is. Let's say, "God loved us and sent."

JOEY: I'll bet I know what comes next. Let me do it. I'll make the next card. (*Exits, mutters, calls out "Nearly ready", etc., and flips over card "trees."*) There. "Trees." "God loved us and sent trees." That's the verse!

JANEY: No, Joey. God does love us, and he did make trees for us to enjoy, but that's not the way the verse goes.

JOEY: Let me try again. (*Exits, mutters, and enters with another card, "rain," which covers the other card "trees."*) "Rain." "God loved us and sent rain."

JANEY: No, no, that's not right! God does love us, and he does send rain to make things grow and provide water for us; but that isn't how the verse goes. Let me give you a clue (*whispers into his ear*). Wanta try again?

JOEY: Yeah, I got it. I got it. Here we go! (*Exits, mutters, enters with last card, "his Son," which covers "rain."*) Why didn't I think of that first? "God loved us and sent his Son."

JANEY: Let's all say it again. "God loved us and sent his son."

JOEY: That's a great Bible verse, Janey. Thanks.

Another idea can be used with Acts 10:38. "Jesus went everywhere doing good." Print the verse on a sign and hold it up for everyone to see. Then, a series of puppets enter one at a time. Each reads the sign, thinks of something good he needs to do, states it, and exits. This process can be repeated as often as feasible.

Bible Story Recall

The following script demonstrates how to use puppets to review children on a Bible story. Two puppets enter, greet the children, and discuss the day's activities.

ONE: I know what let's do! Let's play a game.

TWO: Goody! I love games. What shall we play?

ONE: Guess what?

TWO: Whattaya mean, guess what? I can't guess what game you want to play. Just tell me.

ONE: Guess what?

TWO: Oh, I'm not gonna play with you. You just want to tease. I'm going home.

ONE: Hey, wait! I'm not teasing. That's the name of the game—Guess what? It's a guessing game.

TWO: Well, why didn't you say so?

ONE: I tried. Anyway, here's how it goes. I'll think of something that happened when people met Jesus, and you try to guess what it was.

TWO: Okay, let's go. Boys and girls, I may need some help, will you help me if I can't guess what? Good. Okay, let's start the game.

ONE: I'm thinking of a man who was very short. His name was Zacchaeus. Nobody liked him because he was a bad tax collector. He took more money than the people owed. One day Jesus came to his town. Zacchaeus couldn't see over the crowd because he was short. So he climbed into a tree. When Jesus came along, guess what he did?

TWO: Uh . . . It's on the tip of my tongue . . . I'll get it . . . oh . . . I need help, boys and girls. What did Jesus do? *(Answer: He called Zacchaeus down from the tree so he could visit in Zacchaeus' home.)* Yeah, that's it. I knew it all along . . . well, almost all along.

ONE: And guess what happened after Jesus went to Zacchaeus house?

TWO: Well, uh . . . how about it, boys and girls? *(Answer: Jesus changed Zacchaeus' life. Zacchaeus gave back the money he stole and gave money to the poor.)* Right. Zacchaeus was changed after he met Jesus.

This type of review can be used with any Bible story. The depth and type of questions will vary depending on the age of the children.

Chapter 4
TECHNICAL PRODUCTION

Props and Costumes

The appearance of a puppet can be altered considerably by the use of props and costumes. Hair, beards, moustaches, glasses, clothing, jewelry, and many other things may be added to the basic puppet for character. Other possibilities are: hair bows, guitars or other instruments and hand props, handkerchiefs, vests, shirts, ties, bandanas, purses, and many more items.

One of the best sources of props is a party supply store. Another good source is the toy counter at the local variety store. Here are some ideas that may be helpful. Keep on hand a box of wig or "T" pins. These can be purchased in small, plastic boxes. The pins are useful for pinning on large items such as hats, hair bows, guitars (cut from colored poster board), handkerchiefs, etc.

Another type of pin to use is the dressmaker pin. The colored heads blend well with clothing, yet are easy to find when changing costumes. These are good for securing moustaches, beards, and clothing. When putting on extra clothing (such as an open vest over a shirt), place one or two pins in the vest to secure it to the puppet. Sometimes the puppets become quite active, and clothes do everything except stay on.

When shopping for props, do not forget items such as small, plastic wrist watches, badges of all sorts, plastic party hats (such as derbies or cowboy hats), and other similar items. A puppet can easily wear a pair of eyeglasses. Simply attach a rubber band to each earpiece, and then slip them over the puppet's head.

Some clothing and props will need to be made from scratch. Others, particularly for larger puppets, are easily found in stores. Larger puppets may wear size two or three in children's clothing. These can be easily fitted and adapted to the puppet.

The imagination and creativity of the puppeteer can convert many other items to natural attire for puppets.

Scenery

Scenery enhances a puppet production by increasing the believability of the situation in the script. Therefore, scenery must express some element of the puppet production. Care must be taken that scenery does not distract or interfere with communication between puppets and the audience. Scenery should directly assist and completely support the dramatic action of the puppet script.

Normally, puppet productions are relatively short and the dramatic action of the script is simple. As a general rule, the shorter the script, the less scenery is necessary. In longer productions, scenery creates added visual interest and can be instrumental in maintaining the attention span of the audience.

Unlimited possibilities exist for use of scenic effects with puppets. Simple, fragmentary scenic pieces usually work very well. However, it is possible to use elaborately painted backdrops, projections, specially-constructed items (trees, shrubbery, churches, houses, stairways, columns, etc.), and types of moving scenery.

The imagination of the puppeteer and audience can create many efficient, simple scenic items. A tree for Zacchaeus may be a small tree branch collected near the church. A piece of cardboard may be cut into the shape of a tree and colored or painted to suggest the spot from which Zacchaeus observed Jesus. An elaborate production of the story might have a tree made of papier-mache with detailed limbs and leaves.

Elaborate scenery can be justified if a production is to be presented many times. It is the responsibility of the puppet ministry director to determine if the time and cost of constructing special scenic items are justified.

Cleverly drawn or painted signs work well in short, episodic puppet shows. These can indicate the location, time, or give other information that will help the audience understand the story. Comic effects can be achieved by using multiple signs, signs with arrows, signs with cartoon figures, and signs with cartoon sketches of places. The effect is enhanced if a puppet actually holds the signs. Occasionally, a sign can become a puppet and participate in the action.

Painted scenery can be manipulated like the signs by placing various items on sticks and holding them up. Painted cloths or other types of backdrops can be hung over the back of the puppet stage. Or, they can be pinned or otherwise attached to the back of the puppet stage. Another way to achieve the idea of puppets traveling is to use butcher paper and roll it like a scroll. Scenic elements are painted or sketched on the butcher paper, and the scroll is then rolled from one spool to the other. The paper moving behind the puppets can suggest that the puppets are walking.

Flats may also be constructed by the puppet team and used over and over. A flat is constructed of muslin tightly stretched over a wooden frame. The muslin is sized and painted. It can be repainted many times. Two or three such flats would provide an excellent stock from which to draw scenery for specific productions. One flat might be used to identify the puppet team, and it can be used in every production. For additional information on flats and painted scenery, consult one of the scenic books listed in the "Bibliography."

Fragments of doors, windows, roofs, etc. are often more effective than complete representations. A door frame can easily be constructed from cardboard or plywood. The puppets could walk through the opening to suggest the door. Windows can be constructed in a similar manner and simply hung by wire over the back of the puppet curtain.

Several types of moving scenery can add spectacle to a puppet show. Simple moving scenery like painted cars, trains, clouds, and birds enhance the fascination of a puppet show. Flys and other insects that are generally accepted as nuisances are excellent comic devices when they plague puppets. Another type of moving scenery, the periaktoi, is an efficient way of changing scenes. A "periaktoi" is a three-sided figure with a different scene painted on each side. It can rotate on a shaft either perpendicular or horizontal to the floor. A simple rotation of a periaktoi can change a scene quickly and efficiently.

Scenic requirements are somewhat different for marionettes (string puppets). Marionettes are maneuvered by strings from the top of the puppet stage. The marionette stage has a floor, and scenery must sit securely on this floor. Trees, houses, and other scenery will need to be weighted at the bottom or attached to the stage by some combination of hooks or latches.

Visual warmth is important whenever scenery is used with puppets. Sometimes this warmth can be achieved by paint and light. Sometimes scenic pieces may be covered with flannel or some other material expressing warmth in color and texture. In fact, the entire stage can be covered with cloth to engulf the puppet in warmth.

Some scenic pieces may be discovered at toy store sales and saved for future use. It is a good idea to maintain a stock of basic items. Keep scenery in stock if there is a chance that it, or a portion of it, can by used in a future production. Elaborate and expensive items should certainly be stored for future use.

The best scenic items are those that evolve from the imagination and creativity of the puppeteer. Costly, hard-to-construct pieces may or may not be the best scenic items in the long run. The puppeteer must thoroughly understand the dramatic action of the puppet first, then select scenery that assists and completely supports that action.

Lighting

The basic purpose of all dramatic lighting techniques is to illuminate the performer. The evolution of stage lighting from crude candles and oil lamps to the present-day science has opened up unlimited potential for the use of light in dramatic performances. Lighting naturally illuminates the performer, but the many different ways light can be utilized offers another level of expression.

In puppetry, lighting can be a tremendous addition to a developing puppet ministry. Lights add emphasis to the puppets and their surroundings by highlighting the subjects. Color and intensity of light enhance situation and mood in the puppet play. Lights permit quick and efficient scenic changes as well as add emphasis to entrances and exits. Special lighting can provide many basic scenic effects. Often it is time-saving to use lights to achieve a scenic effect as opposed to constructing and painting special scenery.

The primary problem in lighting puppets is finding equipment that is small enough to efficiently serve a puppet production. The smaller the puppet and puppet stage, the more difficult the task.

Techniques for lighting puppets are similar to those used in lighting full-sized stages. However, there are several notable differences. With puppets, fewer instruments are necessary. It is almost impossible to scale down lighting in proportion to the size of the puppet stage. Lighting instruments that small are simply not readily available. Consequently, the instruments selected must be versatile and do more things. Adequate lighting for a puppet stage may be a home-built system utilizing reflector spotlights and industrial wall dimmers. Basically, lighting the puppet stage is simpler than lighting a full-scale stage. Many special effects possible on full-size stages are simply impractical with puppets.

Modern lighting systems have three primary component parts: a dimming system, lighting instruments, and a patch system to plug instruments into dimmers. For most puppet stages the instruments may be plugged directly into the dimmers, eliminating the patch system.

Dimmers—Several types of dimmers are available for use with puppets. Most of these are electronic dimming systems, often called SCR's. These are available from most theatrical lighting companies (see listing at end of book). The smallest dimmers are generally in the 1,000-watt range, although at least one company markets a dimmer board with six, 600-watt dimmers. This board is ideal for puppets. A 600-watt dimmer is capable of handling six, 100-watt instruments, or any number of instruments whose total does not exceed 600 watts.

An excellent dimming system can be constructed using 500-watt industrial wall dimmers. These are often used in homes, and they are available in sizes from 500 to 2,000 watts. They can be purchased in local stores stocking electrical hardware. The primary problem with this type of system is achieving a master control over all the dimmers. Without a master, enough hands must be available to maneuver all the dimmers simultaneously. A major advantage of the homemade system is cost. Prices vary, but the cost savings over a manufactured six, 600-watt system may be fifty to seventy-five percent.

Most homemade systems will plug into a 110-volt electrical outlet. However, some manufactured systems may require a 220-volt power source. The most efficient system for traveling in and out of the church building should require only a 110-volt power source.

Lighting instruments—A variety of lighting instruments may be used with puppets. Three types commonly used are: individual spotlights, general flood lights, and strip lights. Occasionally a large follow spot can be used to light an entire stage. However, there is little flexibility with only one light source. Individual spotlights may be very small stage lights termed "peewees" or "pinspots." Normally these are fresnels with a three-inch diameter spotlight opening. The instrument contains a light source (lamp), lens (for focus control), shutters (to control the borders of the light), and usually a gel frame (to hold color media). Normally these instruments are hung from a pipe by means of "C" clamps. Reflector instruments do not have focus controls or shutters. However, color media usually can be placed on the instrument. These instruments vary in size, with some available as small as forty watts. These are perfect for puppet stages. Two basic categories of reflector instruments are available: indoor and outdoor. The outdoor instrument has a better lens, but it also costs more. Reflector instruments usually are marketed with a lamp base connected to a clamp. This facilitates hanging the instrument because it can be clamped to almost anything sturdy enough to support its weight.

Floodlights offer a lot of general light, but very little control. The floodlight does not have a lens or shutters. (Some floods may have large blinds that can be maneuvered for limited control of the light.) A floodlight is an inexpensive and simple tool to highlight puppets with light.

Striplights are available in various sizes. Essen-

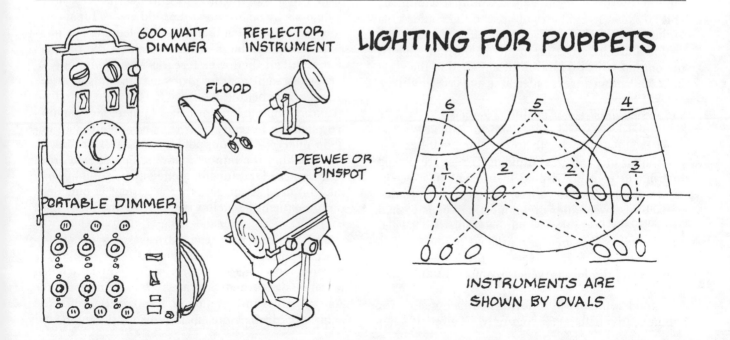

600 WATT DIMMER

REFLECTOR INSTRUMENT

FLOOD

PEEWEE OR PINSPOT

PORTABLE DIMMER

LIGHTING FOR PUPPETS

INSTRUMENTS ARE SHOWN BY OVALS

tially, the striplight is a strip of small lamps (sometimes regular household light bulbs are used) attached to a frame. These offer good general lighting, but they are relatively inflexible. Floodlights and striplights may be used to wash a puppet stage in color.

Lights may be hung from any number of places. A pipe may be designed directly into the puppet stage. The pipe should be in front of the stage and over the puppets. Sometimes the instruments may be hung from trees (light poles) placed in the audience. Trees offer excellent flexibility because they can be placed at a distance providing the most efficiency for the throw (beam length) of the instrument. If trees are used, they must be adequately weighted or mounted to insure that an audience member could not accidently knock them over or otherwise dislodge them. Lighting instruments become extremely hot and must be mounted away from flammable materials.

The angle of light on the puppet needs to remove as many unnatural shadows as possible. The optimum angle is thirty to forty-five degrees to the head of the puppet. Basic lighting technique requires a minimum of two or more lights per area. If two instruments are used, they should be placed so that they will strike the puppet just to his right and left. This angle removes a side shadow that can occur if the instrument strikes the puppet full front. A puppet stage may be divided into three areas (right, center, and left), requiring a minimum of six instruments. Each instrument will be aimed at its particular area, and all light beams should cross as much as possible. This will help give an even spray of light across the puppet stage. A puppet should be able to move from the right area to the center area without passing through a shadowed area. When the center and left areas are dimmed out completely, the puppet will still be well-illuminated in the right area. This procedure is called area and cross-lighting.

Color mediums—Color mediums are used in lighting to emphasize natural colors and to achieve special effects. Three types of lighting color mediums are: gelatin, plastic, and glass (rondels). These are placed in front of each individual instrument in a gel or rondel frame. A wide variety of colors are available in each of the mediums. The most inexpensive and probably the best for most puppet ministries is gelatin. This is a thin plastic marketed in sheets. The sheets are cut with scissors to fit the gel frame. Plastics and rondels are generally more durable than gelatin.

A good principle to follow when using color for the first time is to use it sparingly. Too much color quickly distorts every object it strikes. If such distortion is not intended, the consequences can be disastrous. Light pinks and ambers are very good for highlighting flesh-colored puppets. Generally this combination of color brings out the natural warm tints in puppets and scenery.

Color mediums simply remove varying degrees of other colors from the light. For example, if blue gel is used, colors except blue will be removed in proportion to the shade of gel. When blue light strikes the surface, it highlights blue in the subject. If a puppet is multicolored with some blue thread, a blue gel will distort all other colors from their natural tint. The distortion will be in proportion to the intensity of the blue. As a general rule, color mediums should be mixed to highlight important colors in the puppet production. Experimentation will offer the best insight into particular colors to be mixed with each production.

One color often is used to achieve a special effect. This is termed a "wash." Blues often are used for evening or night scenes. However, if only the wash is used, only the color of the wash will be reflected. Normally, it is best to mix a wash with other colors.

Additional lighting effects—Other special effects may be achieved with lights. Slides projected from the rear of a puppet stage on a scrim can represent scenic effects. If rear projection is used, front lighting must be focused so that there is a minimum of frontal light striking the scrim. In rear projection, simply place the projector behind the stage at a distance necessary to achieve the desired size of picture. Unbleached muslin or other thin material tightly drawn to a frame will work for a scrim.

Lights may be placed at unusual angles for special effects. Foot lighting (below and in front of the puppets) will place large shadows behind the puppets and highlight the lower features of the puppet. Occasionally light may be projected straight up at the puppet from behind the stage to give an eerie effect. (This is similar to holding a flashlight under the chin.) Top lighting (directly over the puppet) gives an angelic effect to the puppet or scenery. Curtains or walls behind the puppets may be lighted and front lights blacked out for silhouette effects. Side lighting may be used to suggest that a puppet is outside a building, or in a shadow away from the main light source.

Small mirror balls can be used very effectively with puppets. A ball (volleyball-size or smaller) is covered with pieces of mirror, mounted where it can be manually turned, and hit by two or more lights. As the ball is turned slowly, a mirror ball effect is achieved. Strobe lights, flashbulbs for lightning, and many other special effects are possible and relatively inexpensive. Regular incandescent lights can be placed in scenery (churches, houses, etc.) to give them warmth.

Adequate rehearsal time with lights is essential to insure proper coordination with the action of the puppets. Fades, either up or down, must reflect the mood and pace of the puppet action. If the show has two or more scenes, use areas of light to isolate different scenes. Lights can cross-fade between areas by fading out the concluding scene at the same time lights are faded up for the next scene. If dimmers are used, check the intensity for each scene. Rarely should the lights be up full all the time. Variety in intensity level increases visual interest in the puppets.

The incorporation of lighting with puppet productions adds an important dimension toward the success of a puppet ministry. Experience with basic lighting techniques will provide the framework for more advanced and involved lighting techniques. Lights that support the action of the puppets increases the attractiveness and professional appearance of the performance.

Tapes and Sound Systems

Puppeteers normally work behind partitions or curtains. Voice amplification improves the verbal communication between puppeteer and audience. The sound system used may be a small guitar amplifier with one microphone or a built-in system with several microphones. Ideally, a puppet team can find a system just to use in its ministry. However, the team probably will have to borrow sound equipment from the music department. As the puppet ministry grows, the need for a personal sound system will become apparent.

Many sound systems are available. Consult a church member or reputable music shop to determine the best equipment for the puppet team.

A puppet production may be presented "live," from prerecorded tapes, or both. If the production is presented live with microphones, it is ideal to have one microphone for each puppeteer that speaks. However, two or more people can use one microphone, provided each person maintains a proper distance from the mike to allow a uniform sound level.

If a permanent system is used as in a puppet theater, or auditorium, it is best to have someone other than a puppeteer to operate the controls. This person is able to listen to the same sound the audience is hearing and, therefore, maintain accurate control of sound levels. It may be necessary to have a puppeteer operate the controls. If this is the case, controls should be adequately lighted and placed so that adjustments may be made during performance.

Prerecorded tapes are very beneficial. Tapes of skits, songs, and dialogues may be purchased or recorded by the puppet team. When the actual voice of each puppeteer is recorded, they can manipulate their puppet more efficiently. However, using any tape allows the puppeteers to forget about speaking, and concentrate totally on the manipulation of the puppets. Tapes can be combined with a "live" performance to add a polished touch. The tapes can lead-in, and lead-out the performance.

Reel-to-reel and cassette tape players can be used. A reel-to-reel player provides excellent quality, but cassette players are more portable and convenient. The best quality of sound will result if the player is patched directly to a sound system rather than allowed to play through a microphone. If cassettes are used, it is advisable to use a different cassette with each song. Counter numbers on tape recorders are not always accurate. By starting each song or skit at the start of the tape, a production can move smoothly and swiftly without any untimely pauses. Both sides of a cassette tape may be used, but it is better not to use both sides in one performance. Rewinding during the performance may be difficult.

Sound equipment is relatively fragile and must be handled with extreme care. Specially constructed crates or trunks should be used to store the equipment for touring. Tape recorders, microphones, and amplifiers need periodic maintenance to keep them clean and in good working order. Certain types of equipment are designed to be more durable than others. This fact should be considered when purchasing any sound or tape equipment.

Singing with Puppets

Puppets can sing at any time, but they are particularly successful at pantomiming with records. This technique is excellent for fellowships and other periods that call for entertainment. Give a puppet a microphone, a guitar, a piano, or whatever, and popular records come to life in a unique and humorous way. Other puppets can be backup groups, or choirs, or special soloists.

Instruments enhance the production if they are available. Use toy instruments, or construct them from cardboard, poster board, or a similar material, and paint them. The hyperactivity of puppets, particularly when they are playing or singing, makes

Personal Scenery and Costume Notes

Performance Comments

(Comments should include audience response to the material covered and the general performance, and a complete performance evaluation.)

a song even more entertaining.

The following list of songs and albums are recordings used successfully with puppets:

"Sing a Song" from *The Official Sesame Street 2—Book and Record Album.*

"Mad" from *The Official Sesame Street 2—Book and Record Album.*

"Mah-na, Mah-na" from *Songs from Sesame Street.*

"There's a Hole in the Bottom of the Sea" from *Songs That Tickle Your Funny Bone.*

"Rubber Duckie" from *Rubber Duckie.*

"Always Leave Them Laughing" from *Rubber Duckie.*

"Alley Cat Dance" from *The Aristocats.*

"This Beautiful Creature" from *The Aristocats.*

"All Kinds of People" from *Mowoli* and *Sesame Street*

"For a Friend" from *Sesame Street.*

"Nobody Knows the Trouble I've Seen" from *Louie Armstrong Treasury.*

Production Checklist

Number of Scenes and Location of Each:

Puppets Required:

Length of Program:

Rehearsal Time Required:

Props Required:

Scenery Required:

Costumes Required:

Sound (Including special effects):

Lighting Required:

Chapter 5
SIMPLE PUPPETS TO MAKE

Spoon Puppet

Materials Needed: Wooden or plastic spoons, scraps of material, construction paper, yarn, lightweight cardboard, pipe cleaners, and clay.

1. Draw a puppet face on the bowl portion of the spoon. Make arms from a pipe cleaner if desired. Cut a robe or dress from scrap material.
2. Make headdress from a small square of material folded in a triangle. Glue headdress to spoon.
3. Or, draw a body for the puppet on lightweight cardboard. Color the body and cut it out. Then make a headdress or use yarn for hair. Paste the body of the puppet to the spoon just below the bowl of the spoon.
4. Manipulate the puppet by holding the handle of the spoon. Or, use a clay base if the puppet is stationary.

Paper Sack Puppet

Materials Needed: Paper sack, newspaper, scraps of material, string, wire, tape, and tube roll.

1. Stuff a small sack (about number 4 size) with a ball of newspaper to form a head.
2. Place a tube roll in the sack to make the neck. Tie securely with a string or tape with masking tape.
3. Draw a face on the sack.
4. Gather a piece of cloth long enough to cover the hand and wrist well and tie cloth to the neck of the puppet.
5. Make hair or headdress as desired.
6. Arms may be made by rolling a piece of newspaper into a roll about ½ inch in diameter and 12 inches long. Insert a piece of medium weight wire in the roll. Secure to the back of the roll by taping in a crisscross fashion.
7. Dress the puppet as desired.

Paper Plate Puppet

Materials Needed: Paper plate, construction paper, small wads of cotton, construction paper, and cloth for costume.

By folding a paper plate in half, the basic element of another interesting puppet is formed. The outer rim of the plate forms a wide mouth, and the fold forms a hinge which allows the mouth to open and close. The eyes are fashioned from construction paper and small wads of cotton. The teeth are made of construction paper glued inside the upper rim of the plate. The costume is made by attaching two pieces of cloth to the plate (one on the top and one on the bottom), leaving sufficient room for the hand to grasp the fold of the plate to manipulate the puppet.

Newspaper Puppet

Materials Needed: Newspaper, wire, tape, construction paper, yarn, nylon stocking, material for clothing.

1. Crumple a double sheet of newspaper to form a ball.
2. Place the ball in the center of an unfolded sheet of newspaper. Gather the paper around the ball to form the neck and body. Holding the paper securely around the head, tape beneath the head to form the neck. Leave the remainder of the paper hanging down to form the body.
3. Roll a sheet of newspaper lengthwise for the legs. Roll another sheet crosswise to form the arms. Tape arms and legs as needed to hold in shape. Insert a medium weight piece of wire in the arms and legs before attaching to the body.
4. Lay the legs across the body about 3 inches from the bottom of the body. Bring the paper back over the legs and tape securely. Fold the legs down.
5. Secure the arms in place by taping in a crisscross fashion around the body.
6. Cover the head with a piece of white cloth. Stretch a flesh-colored nylon stocking over the cloth and secure at the neck. To finish the head, add eyes, mouth, and nose cut from construction paper. Use yarn for the hair. Paint the arms and legs with tempera if desired.
7. Dress the puppet as desired.

Soap Box Puppet

Materials Needed: soap box, scrap cloth, cardboard tube from a coat hanger, tape, glue, tempera paint or crayons.

1. Create facial features with tempera paint or crayons.
2. Construct costume from scrap cloth and glue to box.
3. Tape cardboard tube to box as a means of manipulating the puppet.

Coat Hanger Puppet

Materials Needed: Coat hanger, nylon hose, tape, construction paper, yarn for hair, scraps of material, and paste.

1. Shape the coat hanger to form an oval or a profile for the face.
2. Cut the foot and top off a nylon hose. Tie a knot at one end and pull over the coat hanger with knot at the top and open end at the handle. Tape securely.
3. Cut features for the face from construction paper or felt, and paste on. Hair may be made from yarn or cut from construction paper.
4. Gather a piece of material over the handle to hide puppeteer's hand.
5. Manipulate as a puppet or hold over the face as a mask to help portray a character in a story.

Stick Puppet

Materials Needed: Heavy paper or thin cardboard, stick or dowel, paste, and crayons.

1. Stick puppets are cut out figures that are fastened to a stick or dowel. Draw a figure on heavy paper or thin cardboard. Color the puppet and cut it out.
2. Mount on a stick or dowel about 8 to 10 inches long. The figure can be cut double and the stick or dowel mounted between to give the figure a more finished appearance.
3. Cloth can be glued on finished puppet for clothes.

Flyswatter Puppet

Materials Needed: flyswatter, construction paper, bits of white paper, crayons and glue.

1. Cut facial features from construction paper and glue to the flyswatter.
2. Construct a beard from one solid piece of blue construction paper with tiny bits of white paper glued to it.
3. Add hair, and costume as desired.

Potato Puppet

Materials Needed: potato, scrap felt, yarn, glue, foot-long 3/16 inch dowel, and material for costume.

1. Select scrap pieces of felt for facial features and glue to the potato.
2. Stick the sharpened end of the dowel into the base of the potato 2 or 3 inches.
3. Glue cloth to the dowel or potato for costume.
4. Fasten yarn on top of potato for hair.

Balloon-Tissue Puppet

Materials Needed: Balloon, tissue, spray starch, tempera paint, yarn, and material for clothing.

1. Blow a small balloon to the size of a small orange. Tear some tissue into one-inch strips.
2. Spray balloon with spray starch.
3. Add one layer of the torn tissue. Spray with starch. Continue to add a layer of tissue and spray generously with spray starch after each layer. Add about 8 to 10 layers. When sufficiently thick, pinch in a nose, depress eyes, form mouth and ears. Let dry.
4. Paint with tempera paint, and glue on hair.
5. Roll a cylinder of paper to fit in neck after balloon has been deflated.
6. Gather material for dress and secure around the neck.
7. Manipulate by inserting finger into the neck cylinder.

Sawdust Puppet

Materials Needed: Sawdust, wheat paste, tube roll, drink bottle, tempera paint, yarn, material for clothing, and bowl (for mixing).

1. Mix two parts of fine sawdust with one part of wheat paste. Add water to make the consistency of cookie dough. Roll into a ball.
2. Insert a tube roll into the base of the ball and place roll over the neck of a soft drink bottle.
3. Press in on the ball of sawdust to make the eyes

and mouth. Pull out a little for the nose and ears. Work until the shape is satisfactory.

4. Let it dry thoroughly. Drying may take two or three days and longer if in a damp climate.

5. Paint features with tempera paint. Glue yarn for hair. Gather cloth around the tube roll to form dress.

6. Manipulate the puppet by holding the tube roll.

Child-size Puppet

Materials Needed: Brown wrapping paper, stapler, newspaper, paints or crayons.

1. Child will lie down on a large sheet of brown wrapping paper. Another child or teacher will sketch around the child with a pencil.

2. Cut two pieces exactly alike as the sketch outlined is cut. Staple the edges together, leaving room to stuff with newspaper.

3. Paint or draw the features on the figure. Stuff with crumpled newspaper.

4. To manipulate, the child will hold the figure in front of himself as he moves about.

Fingertip Puppet

Materials Needed: Construction paper, glue, shoe box.

1. Draw a small figure approximately 3-inches tall, or cut a small picture from old literature.

2. For each puppet cut a strip of paper about 1-inch wide and 2½-inches long. Glue the ends of the paper strip together to make a tube. Glue side of the tube to back of the puppet. Put forefinger into the tube and move finger to move puppet.

3. These could be used with a shoe box stage. To make the shoe box stage, remove the lid from the box. Cut a stage opening in the side of the box. Cover or paint the box.

Stuffed Sock Puppet

Materials Needed: cardboard tube, masking tape, cotton sock, cotton, thread, material for facial features, glue, and material for hair.

Begin by making a cardboard tube into which the index finger will be inserted to manipulate the puppet; wrap a 5-inch long piece of cardboard or construction paper around the index finger; adjust it until it fits snugly; fasten the tube together with masking tape. Place the tube in the toe of a man's large, cotton sock. Stuff cotton around it until the head of the puppet is formed. Let part of the tube extend down from the stuffed area to make the puppet's neck. Tie thread tightly around the tube where you want the head to end. Cut slits where the puppet's arms should be. The puppeteer's fingers can be stuck through to form the arms, or simple arms can be sewn on. Sew the costume to the sock, or let the part of the sock not used for the head, be the costume. Features can be stitched, painted, or glued on. Hair can be made from yarn, crepe hair, or crepe paper.

Sock and Glove Puppets
by Sarah Walton Miller

Materials Needed: Sock, glove, red cloth, needle, thread, button eyes, old shirt sleeve, and material for hair (crepe hair, yarn, old wig, or fur).

Perhaps the most expressive puppets are made from socks. By moving his fingers, the puppeteer is able to give the puppet many expressions.

Glove puppets come close to sock puppets in expressiveness. Remember that the thumb is the lower lip in the glove puppet. Sew a dollar-sized circle of red cloth in the palm for the interior of the mouth. Tack the tips of the four fingers together (lest they separate in performance). Sew button eyes about the second joint of the finger. Use buttons with shanks for both socks and gloves for ease of sewing. All parts of both sock and glove puppet should be sewed. Glue does not hold up on stretch fabric. For hair on these puppets, use yarn or pieces of old wigs, or strips of cloth.

Sock puppets, too, use the fully extended thumb for the lower lip. A thumb curled down will not give good expression. Use socks that fit your hand. For women this is usually boy's sizes 6 to 7½; for men usually 8 to 9 or larger. The ribbed crew socks cling to the arm best. For people puppets, the sole of the sock will be the inside of the mouth, the fingers fitting in the toe and the thumb in the heel. For this inside of the mouth, cut a long oval from red cloth, 5 by 2½ inches, or as needed for the size of the sock. Flatten the sock out on a table, with the sole up. Pin the red oval in place on the sole from toe to heel, turning under the raw edge. Be careful to pin only through the sole and not the entire sock. Slip your hand into the sock and hand stitch the red oval into place. Small stitches make the puppet more durable.

To place the eyes, look on the toe for the seam.

Sew the shank buttons in place just above that seam, placing them evenly from side to side. With a felt pen, you may mark the eyelashes and eyebrows. Tack the hair to the top of the head. Hats, jewelry, sunglasses, and so forth, may be added as needed by the character. Costumes for sock and glove puppets are like shirt sleeves. In fact, old shirt sleeves are ideal. The costume may be tacked onto the puppet at your wrist. With a little imagination and a few odds and ends of materials, socks can be made to suggest many animals and characters.

For a sock puppet dog, the sock will be reversed. That is, the sock will be on the hand upside down. The sole will be on top of the hand with the heel over the back of the wrist to represent the dog's neck. Fingers and thumb will all be down in the toe of the sock, which becomes the dog's mouth. Over the entire tip of the toe of the sock, pin in place, as you did the mouth of the person sock, a circle of red cloth 2½ to 3 inches in diameter. Ease in the fulness of the circle, turning under the raw edges and stitching down with small stitches. Then push the circle in, so the fingers become the upper lip and the thumb the lower lip. If you tack at each side of the dog's mouth it will hold in place better. Just above the upper lip, sew a ball-like button or one of the balls from ball fringe. Place the button eyes on the sole of the sock at whatever distance you need for a long or short nosed dog. A cluster of yarn the same color as the sock can suggest a poodle's head. The ears will be two layers of felt sewed on each side of the head. In the patterns are two types of ears: long flop, and perky. From this basic dog puppet you make a lamb, lion, cow and other animals by positioning eyes, changing ears, adding horns or mane and the like.

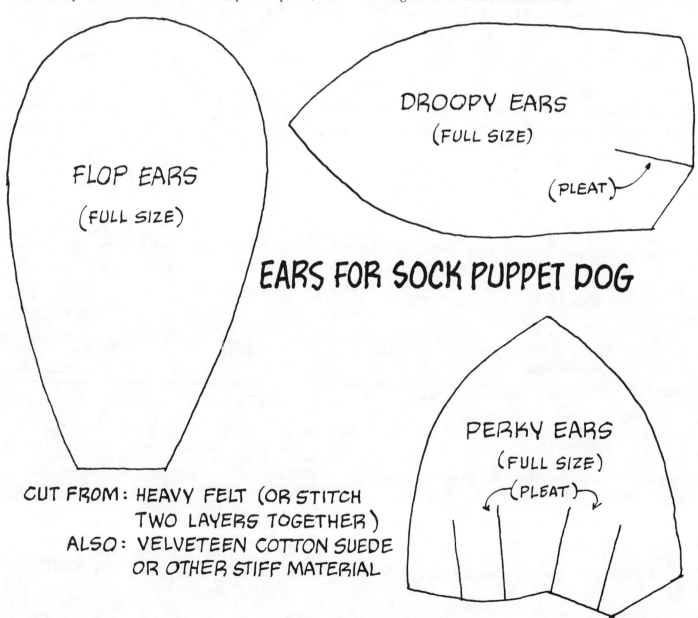

FLOP EARS
(FULL SIZE)

DROOPY EARS
(FULL SIZE)
(PLEAT)

EARS FOR SOCK PUPPET DOG

PERKY EARS
(FULL SIZE)
(PLEAT)

CUT FROM: HEAVY FELT (OR STITCH
TWO LAYERS TOGETHER)
ALSO: VELVETEEN COTTON SUEDE
OR OTHER STIFF MATERIAL

Furry Fellow Puppet

Materials Needed:

Fun Fur-12 or 13 inches wide, and 14 inches long.

Felt-4½ or 3½ inches of a color contrasting to fur color.

Lightweight Cardboard or Stiff Fabric-4½ inches by 3½ inches.

Frog eyes-Any size desired. Razor blade or pointed scissors, pencil, chalk, ruler, thread matching felt in color, needle, white glue.

Solid line shows left half of puppet pattern (A to B to C). Pattern is laid on back side of fur, with side AXX laid along side edge of fur. The top of the fur can be determined by stroking it. It should stroke from the nose end to the bottom, similar to a kitten's fur. With pencil or chalk, draw top arch of pattern A to B at top of fur. Remember, back side of fur faces up. Since pattern shows half of puppet, turn pattern over toward right to make a second arch and continue line down the side so cut fur outline looks like arch one.

Cut from the back side of Fun Fur with razor through backing and pull fur apart. Do not cut between the arches. When the mouth pattern has been cut in the fur as directed, make a felt mouth that is ⅛ inch larger than cardboard. Fur stretches and felt doesn't. After gluing cardboard to felt with tiny edge of felt, extending around cardboard, anchor mouth with pins as illustrated, and sew into opening. Attach Frog Eyes as illustrated (two inches apart and about one inch from top). Fold the puppet, right sides inside. Start sewing at B, tucking stray ends of fur inside, and continue down to bottom. Turn inside out by peeling back bottom.

Mouth Pattern: The mouth is represented on the illustration by the broken line in the oval shape. Make one mouth pattern of lightweight cardboard or stiff cloth. Use this pattern on back side of fur. Top of mouth is 1½ inch from top of puppet, and centered between sides of left half of puppet. On back side of fur, cut with razor, slightly inside of line, making the mouth a bit smaller than the pattern.

FURRY FELLOW PUPPET

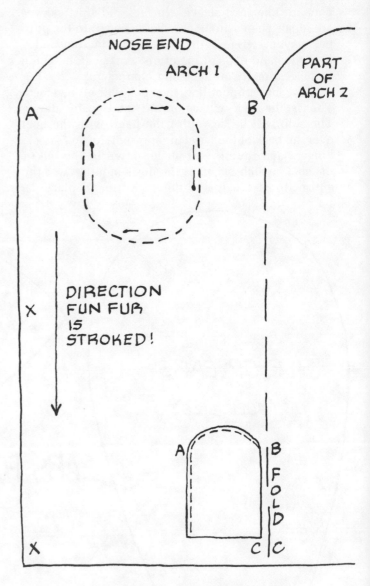

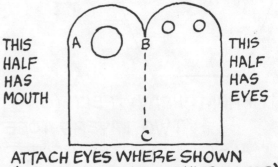

ATTACH EYES WHERE SHOWN
(2" APART AND ABOUT 1" FROM TOP)

Styrofoam Ball Puppets
by Sarah Walton Miller

Materials Needed: Porous styrofoam ball, pencil, latex paint, women's liquid makeup, glue, water, paper, lacquer, poster paint, and yarn, wig, crepe hair or fur for hair.

Styrofoam balls suitable for hand puppets come in 3-, 4-, and 5-inch sizes. The 3-inch size is large enough to be seen in a fairly large assembly room. There are two types of these balls on the market: porous and slick. Buy the porous. Shape the head, not by cutting away, but by pushing and squeezing in little by little. To start the features, mark off with a pencil the general area of the eye sockets and nose, marking the nose wider than will be needed (to allow for shaping later). Push in the eye sockets and along the sides of the wide nose until the right depth is reached. Squeeze the nose into shape, narrowing it and shaping as needed for the character. If you wish ears to show, mark off ears larger than needed. Push in the head and cheeks around the ears. Then shape the ears as desired. For a narrower face, push in the cheeks. Lightly indent for the mouth and chin. If you make a mistake, don't despair. Turn the ball over and begin again.

The next step is to make a hole in the bottom of the head where the neck should be. With a pencil, poke a hole to start and enlarge it until it will contain the index finger plus the neck of the costume (see patterns for Styrofoam ball costume). This hole should be deep enough to reach almost the second joint of the index finger to give the puppeteer control.

At this point the head is ready for painting. Use any good latex wall paint. The dealer will mix a good skin color for you. Or, use women's liquid makeup and mix it with water and glue. For durability, use three layers, letting each dry completely before adding the next. The surface of the ball will still look rough, but is not noticeable a few feet away.

Next, paint on the eyes, lips, and other features. Use poster paint. Instead of painting on eyes, you may draw them on paper and paste to the head. At this point you may spray the head lightly and quickly with lacquer. It gives a bit of durability, but also adds a shine. This step is optional. The head is ready for hair, eyebrows, beard, mustache or anything else you want. Hair may be made from yarn, old wigs, theatrical crepe hair or fur. In attaching anything to these balls, an all-purpose glue is best. The final step is to glue the costume neck into the hole in the head. With the costume on the hand, pour glue into the hole. Push the costume up into the hole as far as it will go. Gently remove the hand. Carefully lay the puppet aside until the glue in the hole has dried, even a day or two.

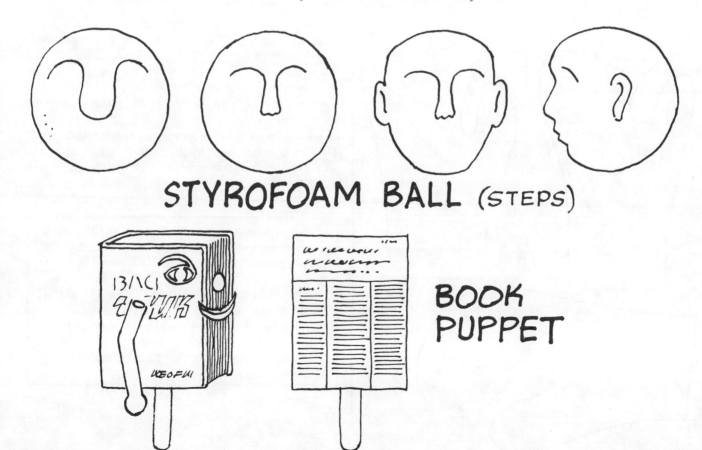

STYROFOAM BALL (STEPS)

BOOK PUPPET

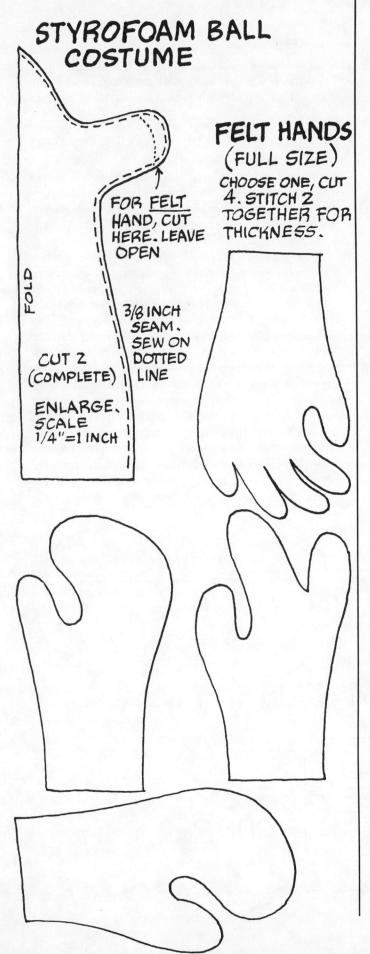

STYROFOAM BALL COSTUME

FOLD

FOR FELT HAND, CUT HERE. LEAVE OPEN

3/8 INCH SEAM. SEW ON DOTTED LINE

CUT 2 (COMPLETE)

ENLARGE. SCALE 1/4"=1 INCH

FELT HANDS
(FULL SIZE)

CHOOSE ONE, CUT 4. STITCH 2 TOGETHER FOR THICKNESS.

Papier-Maché Heads

Materials Needed: wallpaper paste, paper toweling, two tablespoons of dry powder, pint of water, nylon net, and heavy foil or stiff nylon net for the base.

Although papier-maché is difficult to dry in humid climates, it is true that heads made from this material are somewhat stronger than those made from styrofoam balls. This holds true if the papier-maché is thick enough.

Wallpaper paste and paper toweling make good, clean papier-maché. Two tablespoons of the dry powder in a pint or so of water is enough to make several heads. Crinkle up heavy foil or stiff nylon net as the base. Leave a hole in the neck for the finger. Allow the head to dry thoroughly. This may take days. Then paint as suggested for the Styrofoam ball head. Stuff the head with stiff nylon net before gluing in the costume.

Another Styrofoam Puppet

Materials Needed: 6-inch styrofoam ball, 1-foot 3/16 inch dowel, Duco Cement, straight pins, crepe paper, cloth, pipe cleaners, tinsel and crepe paper or yarn for hair.

Use a 6-inch Styrofoam ball for the puppet's head. Sharpen one end of a 1-foot 3/16-inch dowel. Stick the sharpened end (coated with Duco Cement) into the Styrofoam ball. The stick will serve as the handle to control the puppet's movements. With straight pins or Duco Cement, fasten facial features onto the Styrofoam ball. Fashion the hair from crepe paper or yarn. Make the halo from pipe cleaners and tinsel. The costume can be made from crepe paper or cloth. Of course, other characters can be created with the basic Styrofoam ball.

Editor's Note: Several patterns in Chapter 6 are reduced to fit the page size. Pattern parts are in proportion. Enlarge these patterns to fit your specific needs. Place each pattern in an overhead projector and trace the pattern at the desired size on butcher paper. These are advanced patterns. You should have some experience in making simple puppets or puppet clothing before attempting to make these more difficult ones.

Chapter 6
MORE ADVANCED PUPPETS TO MAKE

Foam Head Puppets*
by Kaywin LaNoue

1. Begin with a piece of white foam rubber 4 inches thick. Mark off patterns with a pencil (lightly). If the markings are too dark, they will show through later. Cut with an electric knife, shaping the head, chin, nose, and ears. (Pieces A,B,3 and 8; or 1,2,3, and 8.)

   Note: The nose may be cut out of more narrow foam rubber. You may want to be more creative on the nose using a small Styrofoam ball, a differently shaped foam nose, a felt nose, or decorative foam.

   The narrow foam head number 1 and chin piece number 2 have slits for the hand and thumb. These are made on the back of the puppet only—don't cut all the way through the sides of the puppet's head (see directions on the wide foam head puppet, A and B). The dotted line shows what is inside the puppet—not where to cut. The solid line is the cutting line. Cut slits for the hand and thumb (hand on the large head piece, thumb on the chin piece). Trim and even out the edges and rough places in the foam rubber.

2. Mark and cut the body (number 4 and number 4A—two pieces), arms (foam pieces 10½ inches by 6 inches; cut two pieces), and hands (number 6; cut two). The body and hands should be cut from one-inch foam rubber; the arms are easier to work with if they are cut from the ½-inch or ¾-inch foam rubber. Cut thumbhole in the front piece only (body).

3. Whole Body Puppet. If you are making the entire body puppet, cut out the lower part of the body (one piece—5¼ inches by 7½ inches of foam), one shoe (number 10—cut out of 4-inch foam and then cut in half to make two shoes), and two more arm pieces (foam pieces 10½ inches by 6 inches and ¾ inch to ½ inch thick). The arms and legs are made the same way. Instead of gluing on the hands at the ends of the pieces, make the round tubes and glue them straight onto the tops of the shoes. Dye the shoes black for contrast to the body and they will look like finished shoes. Then stuff the legs as you did the arms, tying off for the knees in the middle, and glue the legs on both sides of the lower body piece. Glue the lower body piece onto the front of the

number 4 piece of foam puppet, gluing the edges together. This will allow the puppet to sit down. (Remember that your hand goes up the back, so you do not need two bottom pieces, just one.)

4. Dye (with Rit dye) all the foam rubber pieces. You may want to cut some other pieces (eyebrows, eyes, cheeks, shoes, etc.) from the foam rubber and dye them at this time. In the dyeing process be sure that the dye is mixed well, using much less hot water than called for in the directions. (Use a little dissolved salt.) Be sure the dye is hot. Heat it on the stove. Wet and wring the pieces before putting them in the dye. Stir constantly, using a wooden spoon. Use rubber gloves to wring the pieces out when they are the color you desire. It will take about three days for the puppet's head to dry. A fan will shorten the drying process.

   Note: The washer may be used to dye the puppets. Don't let the washer go through the wash cycle, but you can let it spin. The dryer may be used to partially dry the puppets.

5. When the head pieces are dry, cut a felt piece 4 inches by 6¾ inches for the narrow foam head puppet's mouth or 7¾ inches by 4¼ inches for the wide foam head puppet's mouth. This piece fits inside the puppet's mouth. Glue the piece in with contact cement. This forms a hinge at the back side of the mouth. Trim off excess felt.

6. The arms and legs may be stuffed if desired. Fold over and glue down the back, making a tube out of the arm foam. Let it dry. (Use liquid latex art form glue, foam craft cement, or contact cement.) Stuff if desired and tie off the tubes in the middle, making an elbow or a knee, and glue on the hand or foot. Lay the pieces aside.

7. Glue back and front body pieces together, being sure to leave the bottom and top open for your arm and hand. Place puppet's arms (folded) between the dots at the shoulders. Glue these on as you glue the front and back together.

   Note: Be sure the thumbs are up and the arm seam is in the back. The foam body front has the thumbhole cut out.

FOAM HEAD PUPPET

8. Attach the head to the body. Place the chin of the puppet (which has a slit for the thumb in the back) right over the thumbhole cut in the front of the body. Glue the top of the front piece to the top part of the head right under the slit for the hand. You can glue the top of the back body piece above the slit in the head piece, but the puppet's mouth will remain open when not in use.

9. Glue on eyes, eyebrows, etc. Long fur, yarn, crepe hair, or old wigs may be used for hair. If you put the hair on with straight pins, you can change it. Eyes and eyebrows can be made from buttons, felt, Styrofoam balls, decorative foam rubber, foam circles, or balls of instant papier-maché with wire loops embedded for attaching to the head with needle and thread.

*From the *Rec Lab Manual,* 1975 © Copyright 1975, The Sunday School Board of the Southern Baptist Convention. All rights reserved.

FOAM RUBBER PUPPET SHOE

CUT 1 OUT OF 4" FOAM
THEN CUT IN HALF, DYE BLACK OR SOME OTHER COLOR BEFORE YOU GLUE.

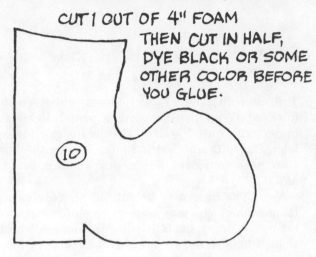

FRONT   BACK

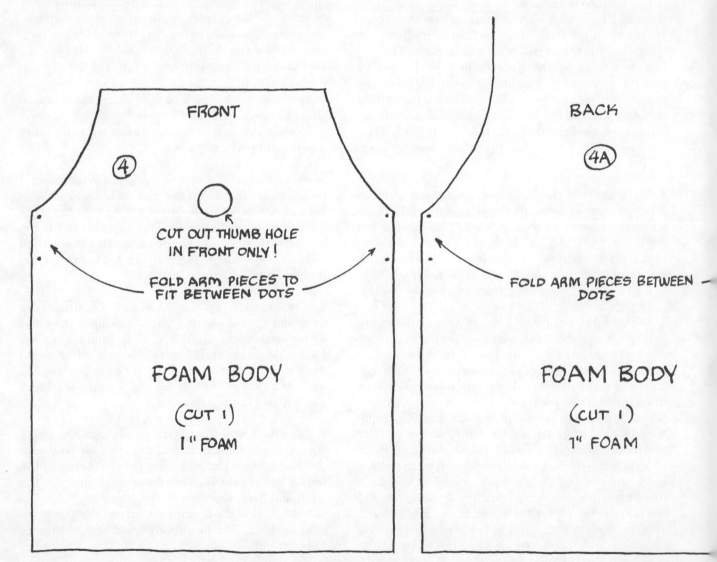

CUT OUT THUMB HOLE IN FRONT ONLY!

FOLD ARM PIECES TO FIT BETWEEN DOTS

FOLD ARM PIECES BETWEEN DOTS

FOAM BODY

(CUT 1)

1" FOAM

FOAM BODY

(CUT 1)

1" FOAM

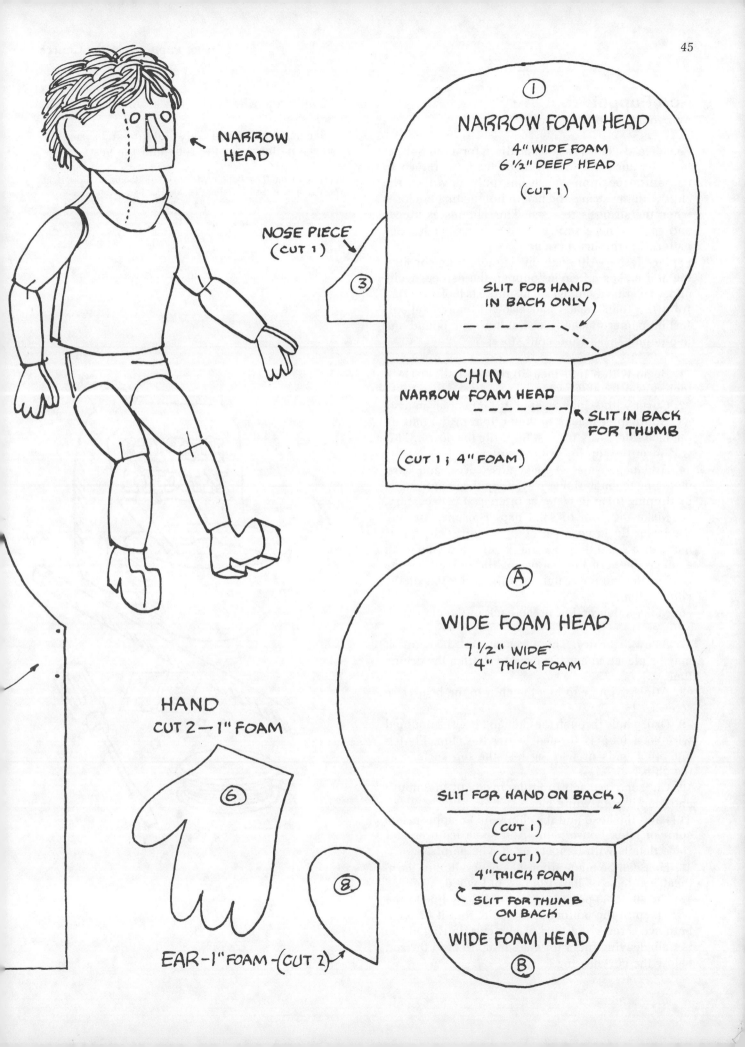

NARROW HEAD

① NARROW FOAM HEAD
4" WIDE FOAM
6½" DEEP HEAD
(CUT 1)

NOSE PIECE
(CUT 1)

③

SLIT FOR HAND
IN BACK ONLY

CHIN
NARROW FOAM HEAD

SLIT IN BACK
FOR THUMB

(CUT 1; 4" FOAM)

Ⓐ WIDE FOAM HEAD
7½" WIDE
4" THICK FOAM

SLIT FOR HAND ON BACK
(CUT 1)

(CUT 1)
4" THICK FOAM
SLIT FOR THUMB
ON BACK

WIDE FOAM HEAD
Ⓑ

HAND
CUT 2—1" FOAM

⑥

⑧

EAR—1" FOAM—(CUT 2)

Rod Puppet*
by Lyn Yarborough

Foam Head—This is a good medium for a rod puppet head because the foam rubber tends to return to its natural position. When one pulls down on the chin with the string, the mouth automatically closes when the string is released. This eliminates hinges and springs, necessary with the papier-maché. See pattern for the instructions.

Papier-Maché—Although this is more time consuming and makes a heavier puppet, the papier-maché offers several advantages. The puppets look different from the foam heads and also are more realistic. Instant papier-maché is available in one-pound and five-pound sacks from craft stores.

1. Begin with a four-inch Styrofoam ball, insert ½ inch dowel for the neck.

2. Cover with ½ inch layer of instant papier-maché.

3. Add papier-maché to the bottom of the ball on the face side, away from or opposite the dowel. This will form the top lip of the mouth.

4. Add papier-maché for a nose, eyes, and ears, modeling the material as clay. Keep the fingers moist by dipping them in water as often as it is necessary.

5. Make the chin of solid papier-maché, forming the lower lip to go with the upper lip. The chin is made as a separate piece and is attached later with a hinge. Be sure the bottom of the top lip, or the roof of the mouth is flat, as well as the top of the chin section.

6. Make a depression in the back of the chin with a finger.

7. Allow it to dry. This takes several days, but it may be placed in a warm oven to shorten the drying time.

8. Attach a hinge to join the chin to the head. Use screws.

9. Drill a hole through the chin and insert a doubled wire so a loop is formed below the chin. Flatten out other ends of wire against the top surface of the chin.

10. Cut some red felt to fit the inside of the mouth and glue it with white glue.

11. Paint the head and the chin with an appropriate color of latex house paint. Add some features and some details with tempera or acrylic paints.

12. Hair can be made from shaggy acrylic fur, yarn, theatrical hair, or hair from an old wig or wiglet.

13. Tie 40- to 60-pound test nylon fishing line to the wire loop in the bottom of the chin. Run it through both eye screws and tie a plastic curtain ring at the bottom, leaving room for one's hand to hold the rod below the curtain ring.

14. Staple a spring to the rod so that it holds the mouth shut.

15. See patterns for rod body and for hand assembly. Also see patterns for the robe and the vest.

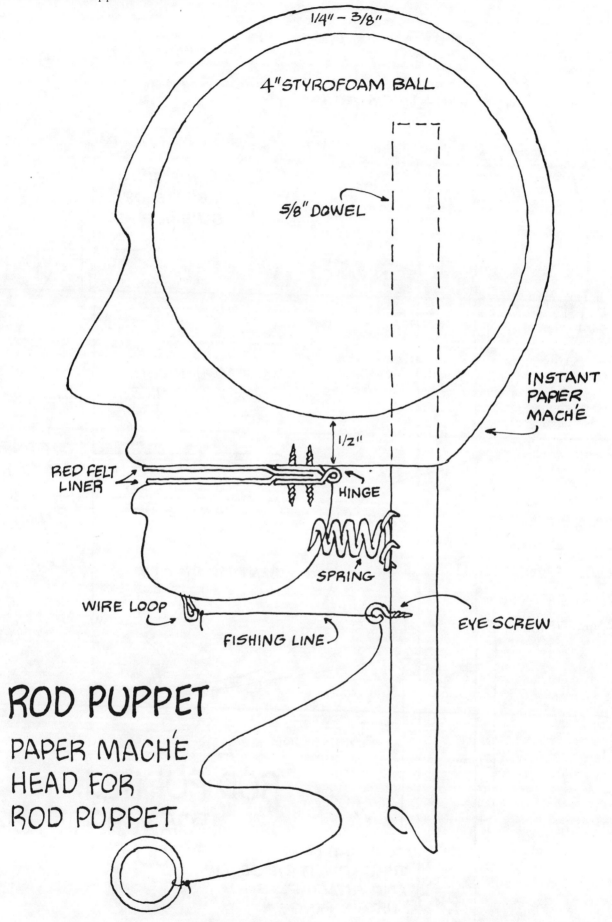

1/4" – 3/8"

4" STYROFOAM BALL

5/8" DOWEL

INSTANT PAPIER MACHÉ

1/2"

RED FELT LINER

HINGE

SPRING

WIRE LOOP

FISHING LINE

EYE SCREW

ROD PUPPET
PAPER MACHÉ HEAD FOR ROD PUPPET

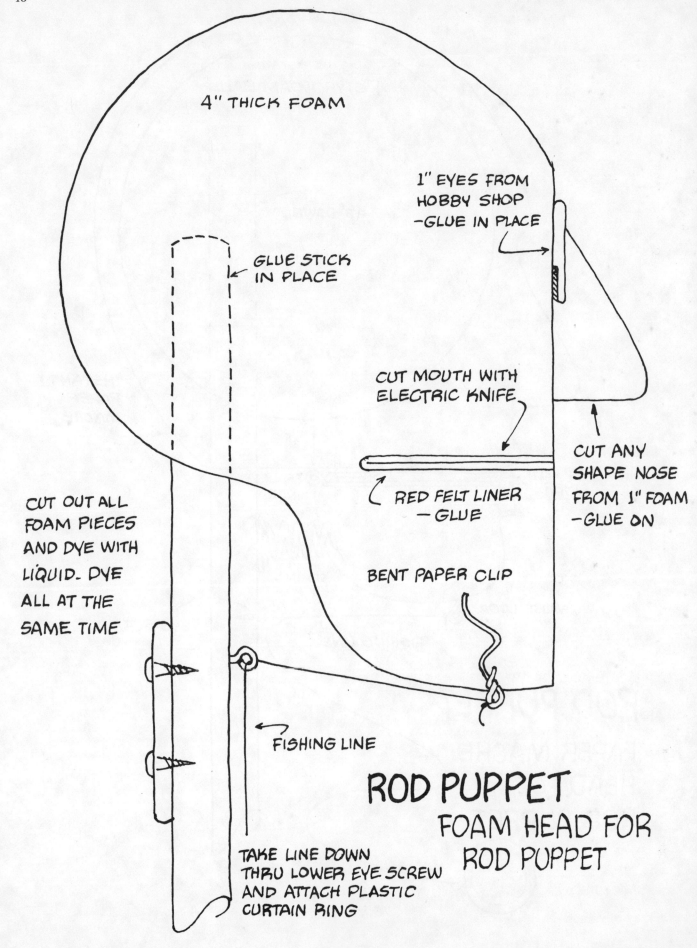

4" THICK FOAM

1" EYES FROM HOBBY SHOP
-GLUE IN PLACE

GLUE STICK IN PLACE

CUT MOUTH WITH ELECTRIC KNIFE

CUT ANY SHAPE NOSE FROM 1" FOAM -GLUE ON

RED FELT LINER -GLUE

CUT OUT ALL FOAM PIECES AND DYE WITH LIQUID. DYE ALL AT THE SAME TIME

BENT PAPER CLIP

FISHING LINE

TAKE LINE DOWN THRU LOWER EYE SCREW AND ATTACH PLASTIC CURTAIN RING

ROD PUPPET
FOAM HEAD FOR ROD PUPPET

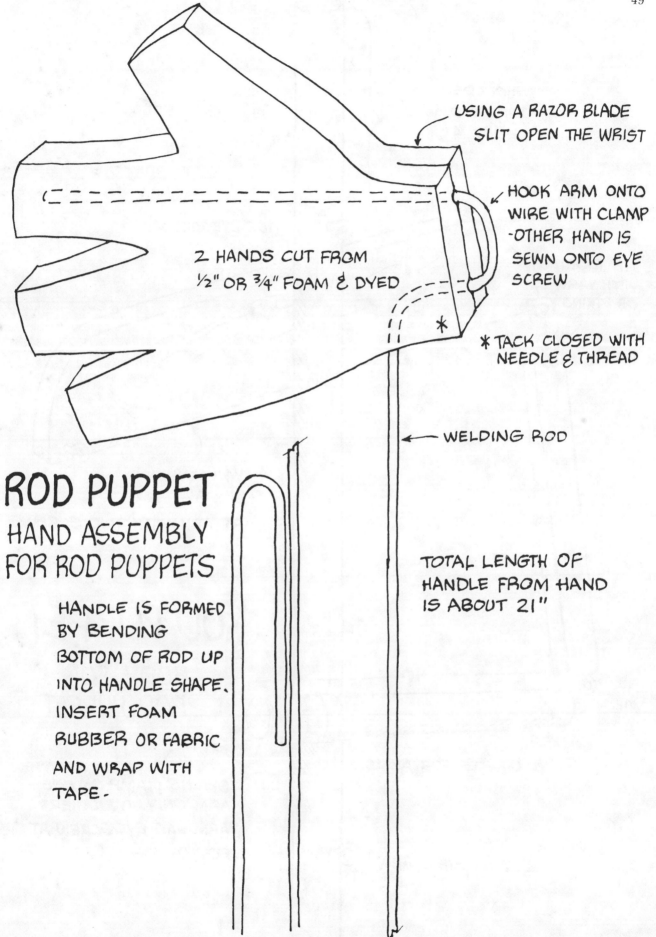

USING A RAZOR BLADE
SLIT OPEN THE WRIST

HOOK ARM ONTO
WIRE WITH CLAMP
-OTHER HAND IS
SEWN ONTO EYE
SCREW

2 HANDS CUT FROM
½" OR ¾" FOAM & DYED

* TACK CLOSED WITH
NEEDLE & THREAD

← WELDING ROD

ROD PUPPET
HAND ASSEMBLY
FOR ROD PUPPETS

HANDLE IS FORMED
BY BENDING
BOTTOM OF ROD UP
INTO HANDLE SHAPE.
INSERT FOAM
RUBBER OR FABRIC
AND WRAP WITH
TAPE.

TOTAL LENGTH OF
HANDLE FROM HAND
IS ABOUT 21"

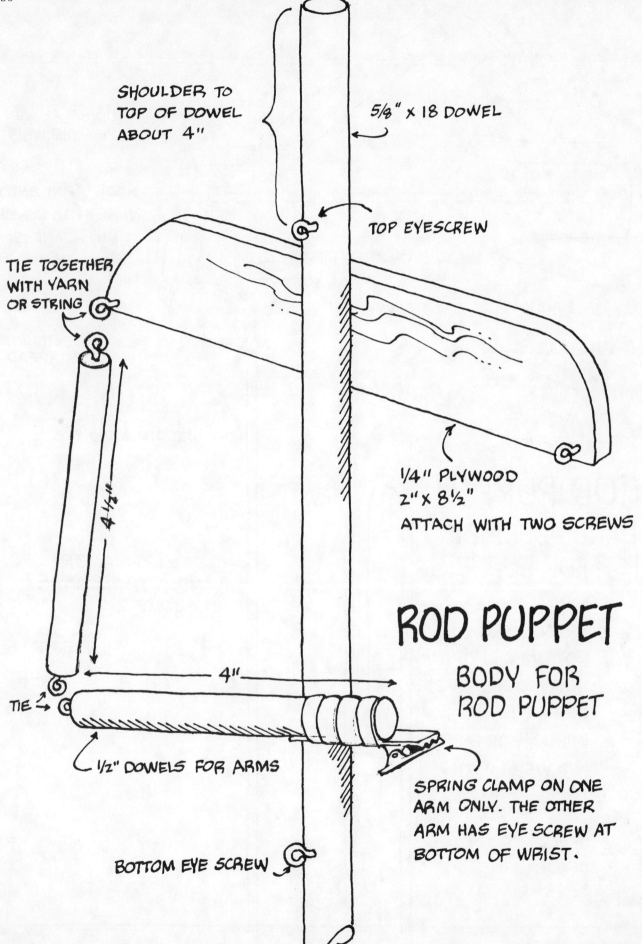

SHOULDER TO
TOP OF DOWEL
ABOUT 4"

5/8" X 18 DOWEL

TOP EYESCREW

TIE TOGETHER
WITH YARN
OR STRING

1/4" PLYWOOD
2" X 8½"
ATTACH WITH TWO SCREWS

4½"

ROD PUPPET

4"

BODY FOR
ROD PUPPET

TIE

½" DOWELS FOR ARMS

SPRING CLAMP ON ONE
ARM ONLY. THE OTHER
ARM HAS EYE SCREW AT
BOTTOM OF WRIST.

BOTTOM EYE SCREW

Costume for Rod Puppet*

by Lyn Yarborough

Robe

1. Robe front and back—Cut 2 from pattern A, placing one on the fold of the material, and the other on double thickness of material. The center line should be nineteen inches long.
2. Sew robe back pieces to robe front at shoulder seams only.
3. Hem center back edges with a soft hem.
4. Sleeve—Cut 2 from pattern B. If trim is desired, sew trim at trim marking. Gather the top of the sleeve. Center line of the pattern should be 11½ inches long.
5. Sew the sleeve to the robe, matching center sleeve marking to shoulder seam, easing to fit. Hem bottom sleeve edges.
6. Sew sleeve seams and side seams.
7. Gather neck edge to desired fit of puppet, and encase in a double fold bias tape, leaving extensions of bias tape in the back for ties.
8. Hem bottom of robe.
9. Sew on snaps, grippers or buttons for back closures.

Vest

1. Cut 2 from vest A. The side seam should be 7¾ inches long.
2. Cut one from vest back B, placing the center back on the fold. The center line should be 10 inches long.
3. Sew vest back to vest front at the shoulder seams.
4. Sew side seams, matching small dots.
5. Encase armhold edges and front edges in double fold bias tape, or overcast edges.
6. Hem the bottom of the vest.
7. If trim is desired, sew it on now.

*Reprinted from *The Puppet Ministry Handbook.* © Copyright, 1974. Puppets 'n' Stuff, Dallas, Texas. Used by permission.

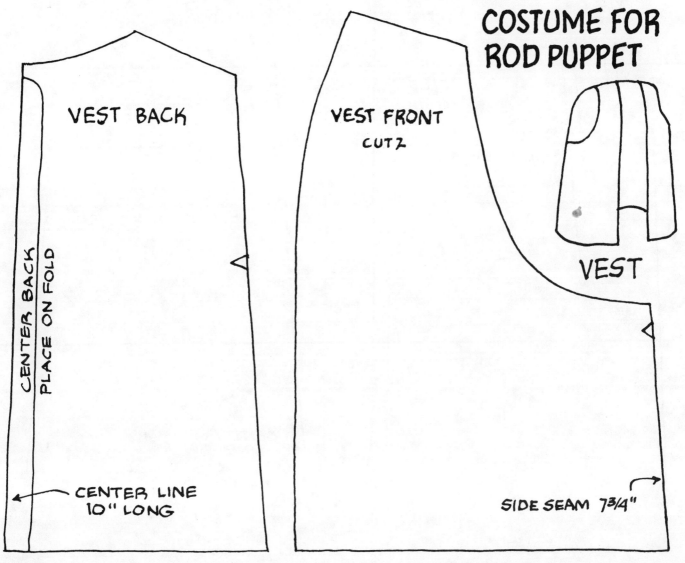

COSTUME FOR ROD PUPPET

VEST BACK

VEST FRONT
CUT 2

VEST

CENTER BACK PLACE ON FOLD

CENTER LINE 10" LONG

SIDE SEAM 7¾"

COSTUME FOR ROD PUPPET
ROBE

GATHERING LINE

CENTER LINE → 19" LONG

(A)

ROBE FRONT AND BACK

PLACE ON FOLD

PLACE CENTER POINT AT SHOULDER SEAM

GATHERING LINE

CENTER LINE

ROBE SLEEVE
(CUT 2)

← CENTER LINE
11½" LONG

Shadow Puppet

Shadow puppets are cutout figures placed behind a screen and lighted from the rear. The screen is constructed of varying types of materials, normally dictated by the size of the screen. If the screen is small, i.e. eight by eleven inches, it may be made of white paper. However, the best screen material is some type of cloth. Muslin or a similar inexpensive material will work.

To make the screen, the fabric is stretched tight until there are no wrinkles or sags. The fabric is attached to a sturdy frame, normally wood or pipe. A facade masks the corners and sides of the screen from the audience. The facade can be imaginatively designed and painted to attract interest to the stage.

The puppets and scenery are cutouts. They are attached to one or more rods and held up behind and against the screen. These can be pure silhouettes. Or, by cutting out certain features, like eyes, they can take on two dimensional characteristics. Painting shadows and certain features will further enhance the puppet.

Body limbs can be jointed by varying types of hinges to enable the limbs to move independently. A rod must be attached to each limb in order to provide controlled maneuverability.

A light source is placed directly behind and slightly above the puppet screen. The light source may be a 150 watt house bulb, a 300 or 400 watt reflector spotlight, or special stage lights. These lights may be placed on a dimmer and the illumination varied for special effects. (The size lamps and type of light will depend on the amount of illumination necessary to project the images through the screen.)

The following illustrations are patterns of some basic figures to be used with Bible stories. Other figures can be traced from pictures, cutout, and used. These puppets may be cut from poster board, manila stock, or similar materials. Figures that are used repeatedly may be constructed from wood. The texture of the material used has considerable affect on the aesthetic qualities of the puppet and puppet show. Experience is the best method of learning what materials are suitable for the specific story being told.

SHADOW PUPPETS

ABRAHAM

TEN COMMANDMENTS

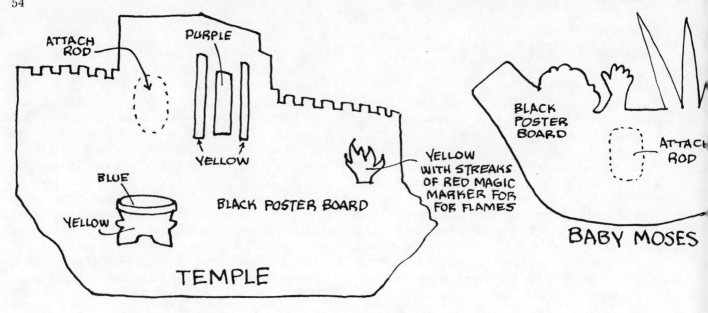

ATTACH ROD

PURPLE

BLACK POSTER BOARD

YELLOW

BLUE

YELLOW

YELLOW WITH STREAKS OF RED MAGIC MARKER FOR FOR FLAMES

TEMPLE

BLACK POSTER BOARD

ATTACH ROD

BABY MOSES

SHADOW PUPPETS

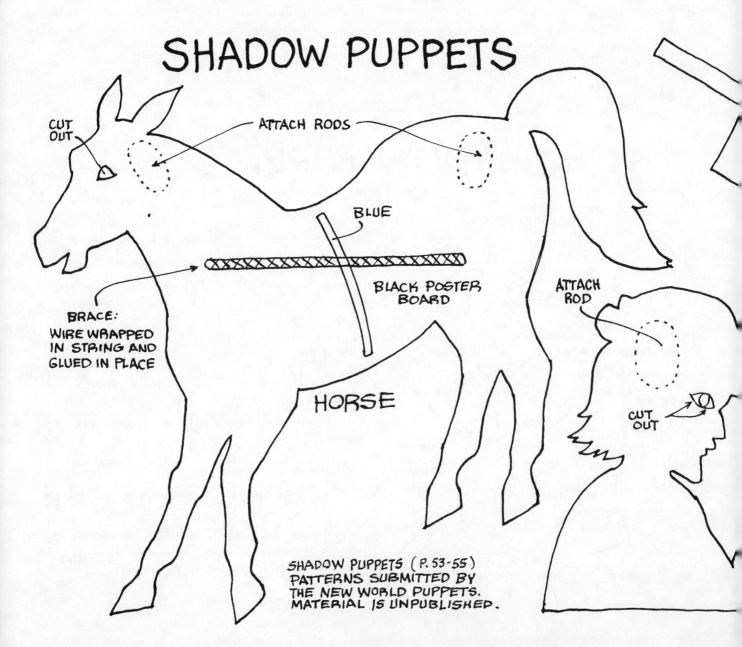

CUT OUT

ATTACH RODS

BLUE

BLACK POSTER BOARD

BRACE: WIRE WRAPPED IN STRING AND GLUED IN PLACE

HORSE

ATTACH ROD

CUT OUT

SHADOW PUPPETS (P. 53-55) PATTERNS SUBMITTED BY THE NEW WORLD PUPPETS. MATERIAL IS UNPUBLISHED.

CUT OUT EYES →
EYEBALLS IN BLACK
INDIA INK.

BLACK INDIA INK

← CUT OUT MOUTH

ATTACH ROD

BLACK INDIA INK

CHILD
OF MANILA
STOCK

CONNECT ROD

CUT FROM
BLACK POSTER
BOARD

CAMEL

BLACK POSTER BOARD

ATTACH ROD

ARK

ATTACH ROD

CUT OUT FROM
BLACK POSTER BOARD

SANHEDRIN

MEMBERS OF THE COUNCIL

A Large Muppet

by Carroll Brown

Materials Needed: (To construct 4 puppets)

1. Two yards of 48-inch wide material. Flesh-colored flannel, or some thicker, washable material is recommended.

2. One-half yard of red felt for mouths.

3. Posterboard for mouth, ½ yd. stitchwitchery.

4. Large glue-on eyes. (These are available in most department stores.)

5. Wigs (½ yard Velcro or a similar material for removable wigs).

6. One-half yard of 60-inch wide fake fur for four wigs. One skein of cotton rug yarn makes two wigs.

7. Two bags of shredded foam rubber to stuff arms, ears, nose, and head.

8. Three-fourth inch thick foam rubber for shoulder padding and chin.

9. Wire for arms (umbrella staves).

10. Lining for head stuffing. Any material will do.

11. Fabric glue.

12. Pipe cleaners for fingers.

Directions:

Make all seams narrow.

1. *Nose* — Place right sides together and sew along dotted lines. Turn and stuff with shredded foam. A pom-pom or embroidery stitch may be substituted.

2. Place the nose on the head front, ½" above the seam line on the right side of fabric and pin. Sew dart A to B on wrong side.

3. Place head front, right side to table, completely open. Place chin piece in same direction, directly under the head front. Do not attach in any way yet.

4. *Mouth-pattern pieces* — Cut one from posterboard, cut two from felt, and cut two from stitchwitchery that adheres to both sides of fabric. Open the posterboard flat and lay a piece of stitchwitchery on top; then a piece of felt. Take a damp cloth and place over the felt. Place a hot iron on the cloth, moving it very slowly. Follow the same procedure for the opposite side.

5. Lay mouth out flat with the inside of the mouth being face down. Find center, top, and bottom of mouth and pin (right sides together) top center of mouth to B on head front and pin bottom center to C on chin. Continue pinning around mouth until it is completely attached (to corners) to the head front and chin. There will be excess fabric at mouth corners, so make a seam connecting DE of head front to FG of chin (both sides of mouth). Mouth should then be pinned at points E and F, fitting snugly to complete the mouth attachment. Seam around the mouth and trim closely. Now the head front, mouth, and chin are connected.

6. Seam back of head together, H to I.

7. *Ears* — Place right sides together, seam on dotted lines, turn, and stuff. Pin ears 1½" above the mouth on head front with tips of ears pointing toward the mouth.

8. With right sides together, attach head front at J to back of head at H. Seam front (face) section to back of head section.

9. With right sides of body together, seam shoulders, K to L.

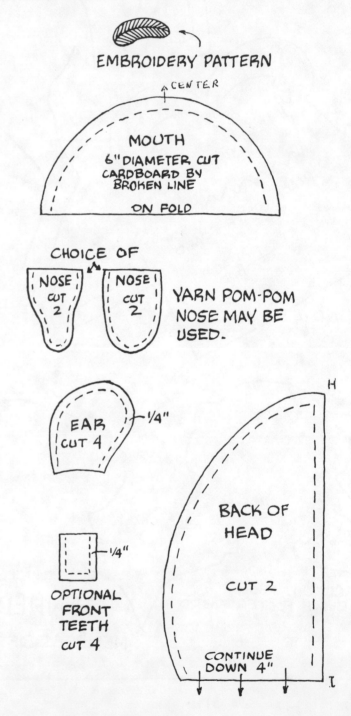

EMBROIDERY PATTERN

↑CENTER

MOUTH
6" DIAMETER CUT CARDBOARD BY BROKEN LINE
ON FOLD

CHOICE OF

NOSE CUT 2   NOSE CUT 2

YARN POM-POM NOSE MAY BE USED.

EAR CUT 4   ←¼"

OPTIONAL FRONT TEETH CUT 4   ←¼"

H

BACK OF HEAD

CUT 2

CONTINUE DOWN 4"

I

10. Attach neck of body to bottom of the chin—right sides together.

11. *Arms* — Place right sides together, seam, and turn. Place pipecleaners the full length of each finger. Bend pipecleaners (at tip) before inserting. Stuff with shredded foam to center fold and seam across for elbow and continue stuffing to complete arm.

12. Connect arm to body by seaming K to M.

13. Seam head lining (right sides together) leaving 2" opening to turn and stuff with shredded foam. Stitch opening by hand. Insert in head.

14. Cut solid ¾" foam for chin and shoulders by dotted lines on patterns and place in puppet (without glue).

15. *Legs* — Place right sides together, seam, and stuff. Attach to puppet's clothing.

16. Wigs and eyebrows can be made from yarn or fake fur. Attach with Velcro.

17. Umbrella staves can be attached to arms by pipecleaners.

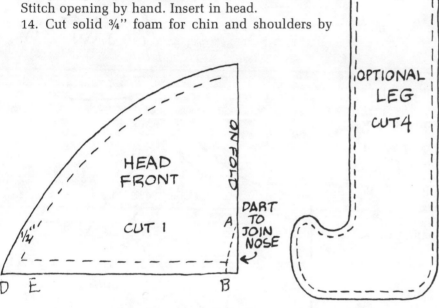

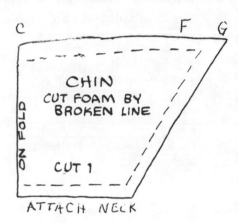

A LARGE MUPPET

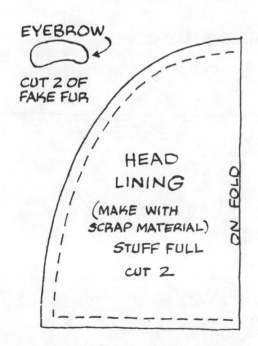

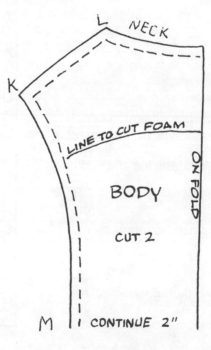

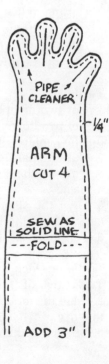

Turtle and Duck Pattern
by Joan King

(Fake fur recommended for this pattern.)

Turtle
End of Egg Mold—Cut the end off the egg mold to allow arms to enter the shell.
Shell Cover—Cut one of this pattern and place the center line on the fold of the material.
Darts—Sew the two darts. Remember to cut out the center of the darts.
Outer Edge of Pattern—Fold under and glue to the ceramic egg mold.

Turtle Stomach
1. Cut one lining and one stomach pattern. Remember to place it on the fold.
2. Stitch the stomach to the stomach lining along the seam line and reverse.
3. Stuff it with polyester fiber.
4. Stitch the area along BAB.
5. Stitch the stomach to the shell from point B to point C.
6. The eyes may be made by gluing black pupils made of black polyester circles to round ball-shaped buttons.

Turtle Arm
1. Cut four of this pattern.
2. Stitch along the seam and reverse.

Mouth
1. Cut one of this pattern.
2. Cut one felt interfacing.
3. Cut one lining.
4. Cut one of top mouth pattern.
5. Cut one of lower jaw pattern.

Turtle Hat
1. Cut two of this pattern.
2. Cut two flowers and cut around piece of material for the center of the flowers and glue in the center.
3. Cut one hat flower stem.
4. Turn up the 3-pointed edges of the hat and make a seam.
5. Glue the stem to the hat and glue a flower to each side of the stem.
6. Felt material is suggested for this pattern.

Turtle or Duck Body
1. Cut two of this pattern.
2. Glue the mouth to the felt mouth interfacing. Let this dry.
3. Stitch together the head front seams and then the head back seams.
4. Stitch mouth OPO to the top mouth.
5. Stitch mouth OSO to the lower jaw.
6. Stitch the beak to the head.
7. Add the eyes.
8. Add the hat to the turtle and then place a bonnet or hat on the duck.
9. Attach the arms to the turtle and stitch the back of the neck to the top of the shell.

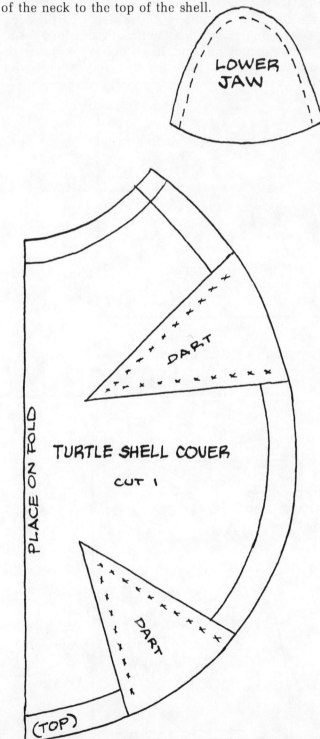

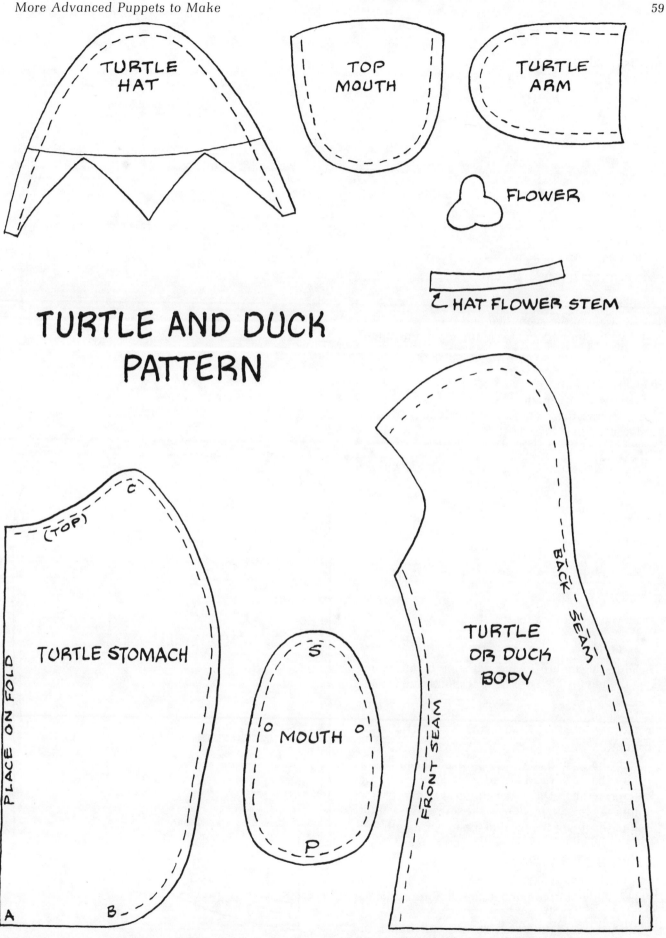

TURTLE HAT

TOP MOUTH

TURTLE ARM

FLOWER

HAT FLOWER STEM

TURTLE AND DUCK PATTERN

TURTLE STOMACH

PLACE ON FOLD

(TOP)

C

A

B

MOUTH

S

O

O

P

TURTLE OR DUCK BODY

BACK SEAM

FRONT SEAM

Bear Pattern
by Joan King

(Fake fur recommended for this pattern.)

Bear Side Head
1. Cut two of this pattern.
2. Clip the dart at point F.
3. Sew the dart at point D.

Bear Lower Jaw
1. Cut one of this pattern.
2. Sew two darts near point O.

Bear Nose
1. Cut two of this pattern.
2. Stitch along the seam line and reverse.
3. Leave the unmarked area at the top of the pattern open to stuff. Stitch this by hand to close.

Bear Front
1. Cut one of this pattern.
2. Sew along the dotted line areas when stitching to side head and back head.

Bear Mouth
1. Cut one of this pattern.
2. Cut one felt interfacing (two felts for more body).
3. Cut one lining.

Bear Ear
1. Cut four of this pattern.
2. Stitch along the seam line and reverse.

Bear Back Head
1. Cut one of this pattern.

Assembling the Bear Pattern
 1. Glue the mouth to the felt mouth interfacing. Glue the mouth lining to the felt mouth interfacing. Let this dry.
 2. Make all darts.
 3. Join the side heads matching AB to AB.
 4. Join the side head CAC to the front head CAC.
 5. Join the side head CD to the front head CD.
 6. Join the back head DD to the front head DD.
 7. Join the back DE to the side head DE.
 8. Join the lower jaw FOF to the lower mouth FOF.
 9. Join the top of the head to the upper mouth FPF.
10. Join the side head FZ to the lower jaw FZ.
11. Stuff the head where it is necessary with polyester fiber.
12. Attach the sleeve.
13. Attach the nose.
14. Attach the ears along a curve.
15. Add the eyes. They may be bought at a craft store.

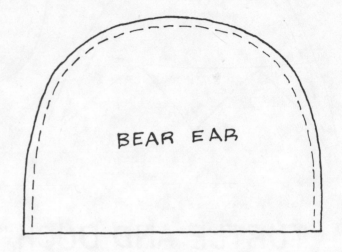

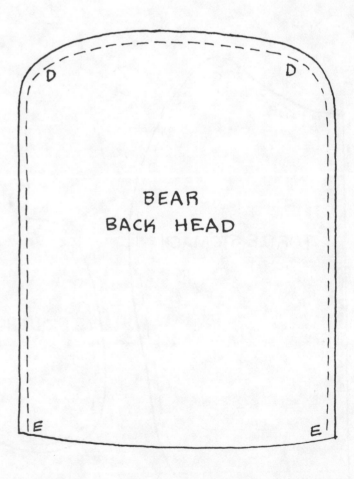

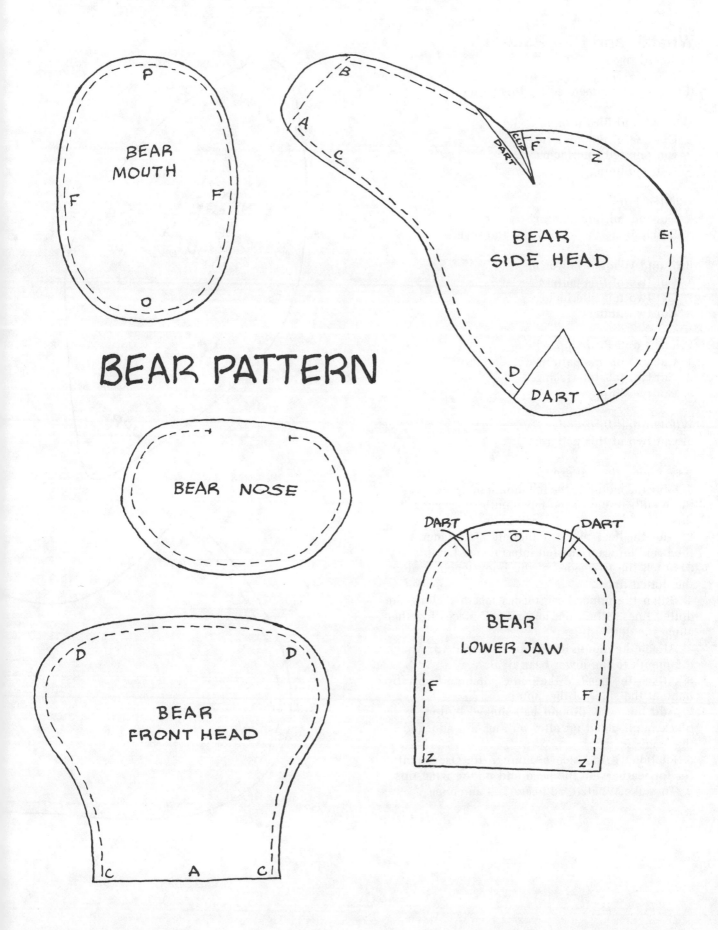

BEAR
MOUTH

P

F

F

O

B

A

C

CLIP

DART

F

Z

BEAR
SIDE HEAD

E

D

DART

BEAR PATTERN

BEAR NOSE

DART

DART

O

BEAR
LOWER JAW

F

F

Z

Z

D

D

BEAR
FRONT HEAD

C

A

C

Whatzit and Bird Pattern
by Joan King

(Fake fur recommended for this pattern.)

Whatzit and Bird Mouth
1. Cut one of this pattern.
2. Cut one felt interfacing.
3. Cut one lining.

Whatzit Ears
1. Cut four of this pattern.
2. Stitch along the seam lines and reverse.

Bird and Whatzit Lower Beak
1. Cut two of this pattern.
2. Cut two felt interfacings.
3. Cut two linings.

Whatzit and Bird Upper Beak
1. Cut two of this pattern.
2. Cut two felt interfacings.
3. Cut two linings.

Whatzit and Bird Body
1. Cut two of this pattern.

Assembling the Pattern
1. Glue the mouth to the felt mouth interfacing. Glue the mouth lining to the felt mouth interfacing. Let this dry.
2. Glue the beak pieces to the felt interfacings. Glue the beak linings to the felt interfacings. Let this dry.
3. Stitch the two sides of the body together along the dotted lines.
4. Stitch the upper beak pieces together along the dotted lines. Stitch the lower beak pieces together along the dotted lines.
5. Attach the mouth to the upper beak BAB. Attach the mouth to the lower beak BCB.
6. Attach the beak to the body, stitching firmly by hand at the sides of the mouth.
7. Add the eyes. (Round ball-shaped buttons with black pupil glued on after buttons are attached to the head.)
8. (Optional) Add sleeve number 1B. Use fanciful fur for feathers on the head and on the wing tips.
9. To make Whatzit, add ears and antennae.

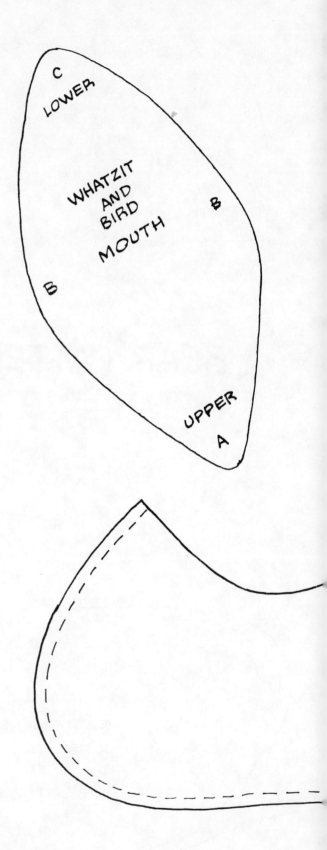

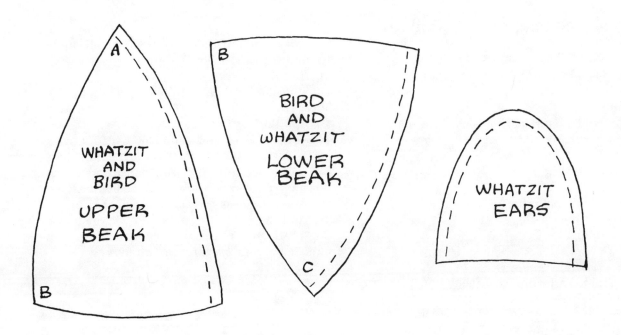

WHATZIT AND BIRD PATTERN

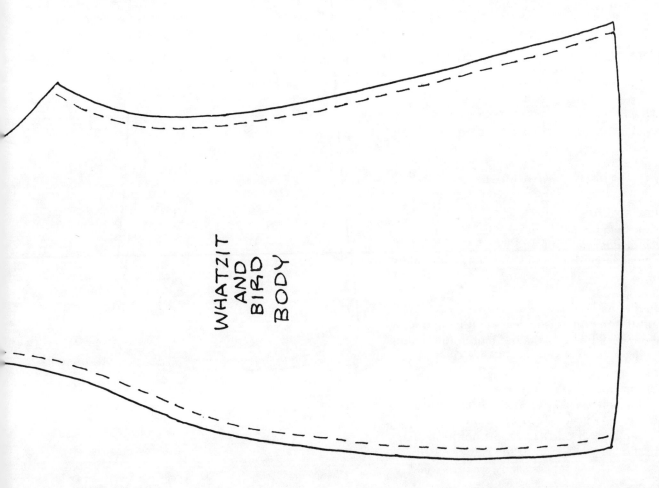

Cow, Goat, Skunk, or Dog Pattern
by Joan King

(Fake Fur recommended for this pattern.)

Side Head
1. Cut two of this pattern. This is used for the cow, goat, skunk, or the dog.
2. Sew darts.

Mouth
1. Cut one of this pattern.
2. Cut one felt interfacing.
3. Cut one lining.

Nose
1. Use this pattern for the cow, goat, and the dog. Cut two of this pattern.
2. Cut this pattern much smaller or use fringe pompom for the skunk's nose.
3. Stitch along the dotted lines leaving the unmarked area open for stuffing.
4. Stuff and reverse.
5. Hand stitch the open area.

Goat or Cow Horn
1. Cut four of this pattern. Sew and reverse.
2. Stuff with polyester fiber.

Lower Jaw
1. Cut one of this pattern.
2. Sew the darts.

Front Head
1. Cut one of this pattern. (white for skunk)

Back Head
1. Cut one of this pattern. (white for skunk)

Goat or Cow Ears
1. Cut four of this pattern.
2. Stitch at the seam line and reverse.
3. Cut much larger for the dog. Cut the pattern about half this size for the skunk.

Assembling the Pattern
1. Glue the mouth to the felt mouth interfacing. Glue the mouth lining to the felt mouth interfacing. Let this dry.
2. Make the darts.
3. Join the side heads AB to AB.
4. Join the side head CAC to the front head CAC.
5. Join the side head CD to the front head CD.
6. Join the back head DD to the front head DD.
7. Join the back head DE to the side head DE.

8. Join the lower jaw FOF to the mouth FOF.
9. Join the top of the head to the mouth FBF.
10. Join the side head FZ to the lower jaw FZ.
11. Add the sleeve.
12. Stuff the head with pillow made with polyester fiber.
13. Add the nose.
14. Add the eyes and ears. Dog eyes are made of black ovals topped with white oval rims. Lids are half ovals cut from fur with nap to create lashes. (Plastic eyelashes may also be glued behind the eyes.)
15. Add the horns for the goat and the cow.
16. Add the wrinkles for the dog. Wrinkles on the dog are made from two rectangular pieces of fur attached across the forehead on curves.

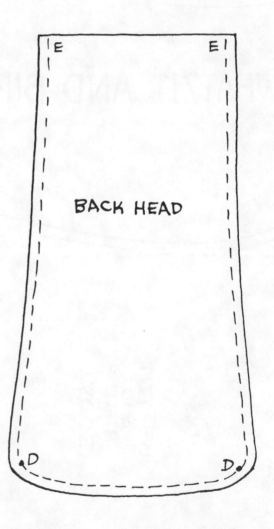

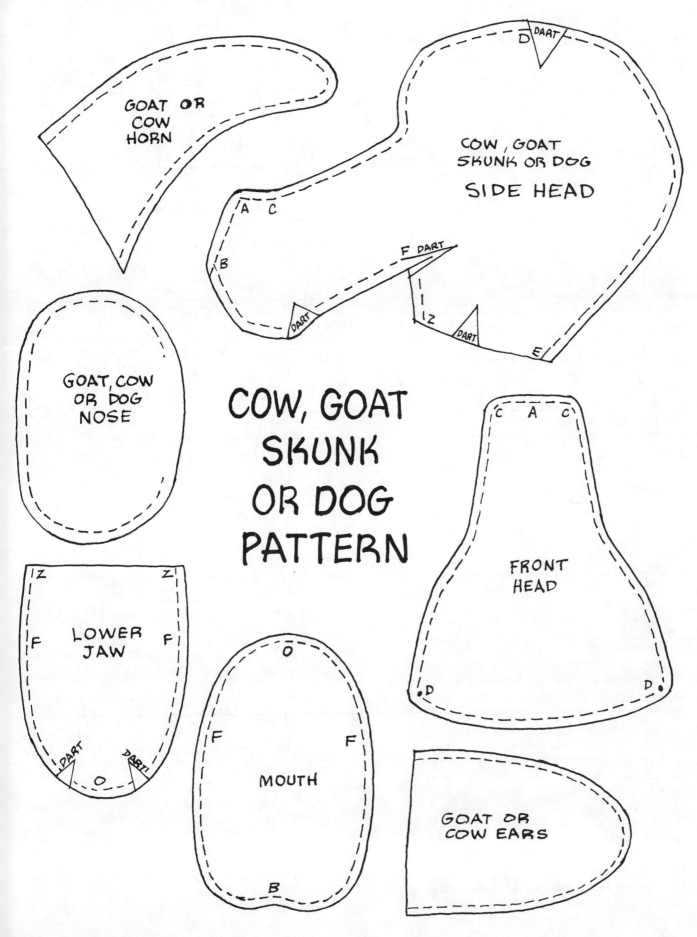

GOAT OR COW HORN

COW, GOAT SKUNK OR DOG SIDE HEAD

D DART

A C

B

F DART

Z

DART

E

GOAT, COW OR DOG NOSE

COW, GOAT SKUNK OR DOG PATTERN

C A C

FRONT HEAD

D D

Z Z

F LOWER JAW F

DART DART

O

O

F F

MOUTH

B

GOAT OR COW EARS

Moose, Giraffe, and Horse Pattern
by Joan King

(Fake fur recommended for this pattern.)

Mouth
1. Cut one of this pattern.
2. Cut one felt interfacing.
3. Cut one lining.

Giraffe Antlers
1. Cut four of this pattern.
2. Sew, reverse, and stuff.

Moose Ears
1. Cut four of this pattern.
2. Stitch on the dotted lines.
3. Make the ears more narrow for the horse and the giraffe.

Front for Moose, Giraffe, and Horse (cut one)

Moose Antlers
1. Cut four of this pattern (off-white polyester material).
2. Sew and reverse.
3. Stuff with polyester fiber.

Side Head
1. Cut two of this pattern.
2. Sew darts.

Back Head
1. Cut one of back head pattern.

Lower Jaw
1. Cut one of this pattern.
2. Sew darts.

Assembling the Pattern
1. Glue the mouth to the felt mouth interfacing. Glue the mouth lining to the felt mouth interfacing. Let this dry.
2. Make the darts.
3. Join the side heads AB to AB.
4. Join the side head CAC to the front head CAC.
5. Join the side head CD to the front head CD.
6. Join the back head DD to the front head DD.
7. Join the back head DE to the side head DE.
8. Join the lower jaw FOF to the mouth FOF.
9. Join the top head to the upper mouth FBF.
10. Join the side head FZ to the lower jaw FZ.
11. Add the sleeve.
12. Stuff the head with pillow made with polyester fiber.

13. Add two nostrils (black fringe balls).
14. Add ears and eyes.
15. Add antlers or mane where it is necessary.

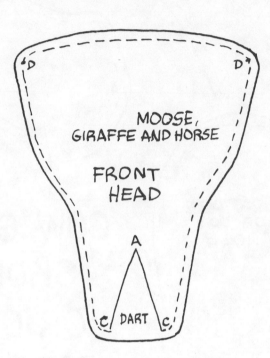

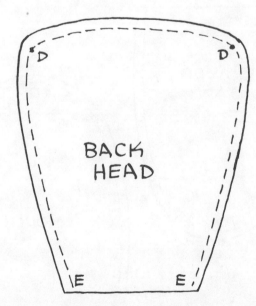

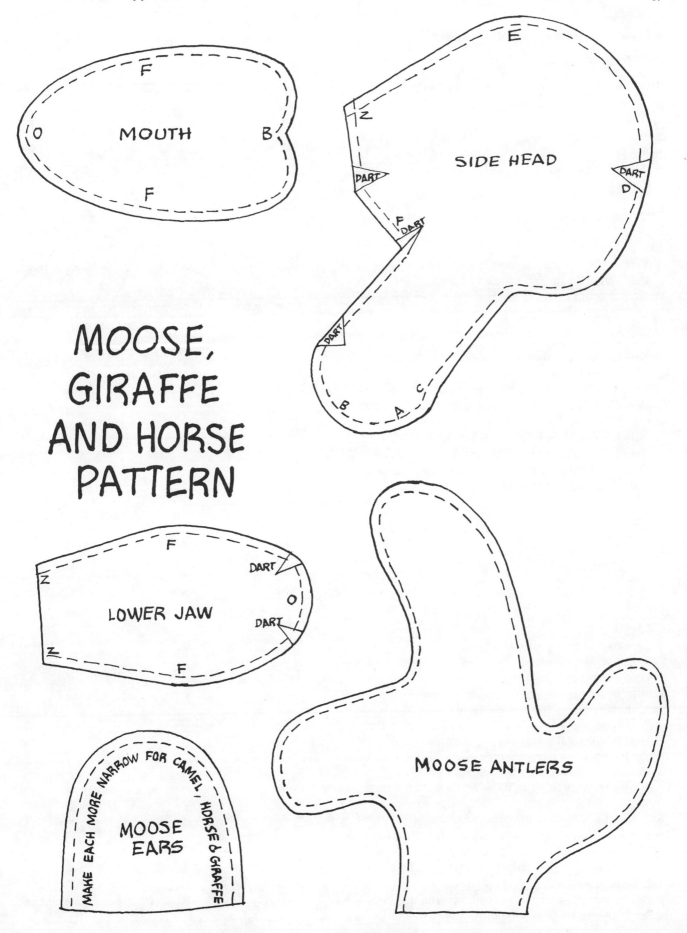

MOUTH

SIDE HEAD

MOOSE, GIRAFFE AND HORSE PATTERN

LOWER JAW

MOOSE ANTLERS

MAKE EACH MORE NARROW FOR CAMEL, HORSE & GIRAFFE

MOOSE EARS

Skunk and Camel Pattern
by Joan King

(Fake fur recommended for this pattern.)

Skunk Head
1. Use the same pattern given for the previous skunk head pattern.
2. Make the pattern smaller—just large enough to fit the hand.

Skunk Nose (Use a small ball from fringe.)

Skunk Tail
1. Cut two of this pattern (black).
2. Cut a strip 3½ inches wide and length of the seam. Attach it around the black front and the back tail to form the side tail (white).

Skunk Body
1. Cut two of this pattern.
2. Cut along line B1, I1, H.
3. Cut a strip of white fur to make a stripe the length of B1, I1, H. Widen the strip from B1 to H. (Two to four inches)
4. Stitch from H to F. Stitch from A to C.
5. From A to B leave open to attach the head. From C to D leave open for arm to operate the puppet.
6. Attach head. Stitch from E to F.
7. Stuff body with a pillow made with polyester fiber.
8. Stuff tail with polyester fiber and stitch to body by hand.

Camel Head (Use the same pattern given for the moose head in previous pattern.)

Camel Tail
1. Cut two of this pattern.
2. Stitch along the seam lines and reverse.

Camel Body
1. Cut two of this pattern along line B, I, G, H.
2. Stitch along the dotted lines. Leave open from A to B to attach the head. From points C to D leave open for arm to operate puppet.
3. Attach the head. Stitch from E to F.
4. Stuff the body with a pillow made with polyester fiber. Add tail.
5. To make a saddle for the camel use a different material of cotton blend, attaching from points G to H and over the hump. The saddle may be trimmed with rickrack or other colored trimming. The saddle can be made any size.
6. Make harness with rickrack or other colored trimming and sew to head attaching reigns to saddle.

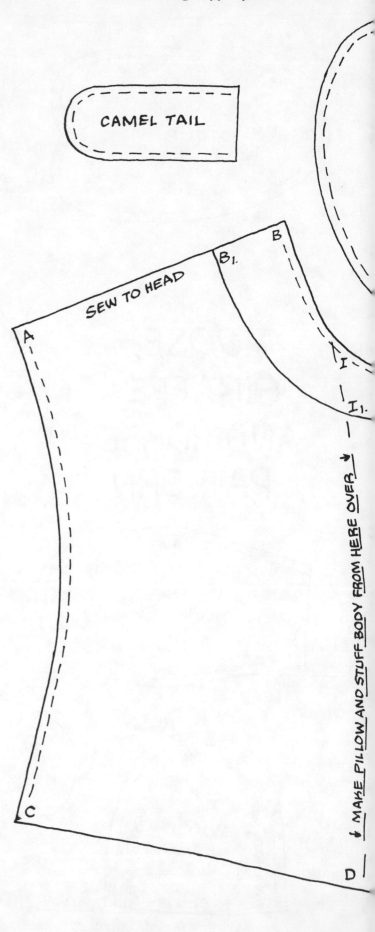

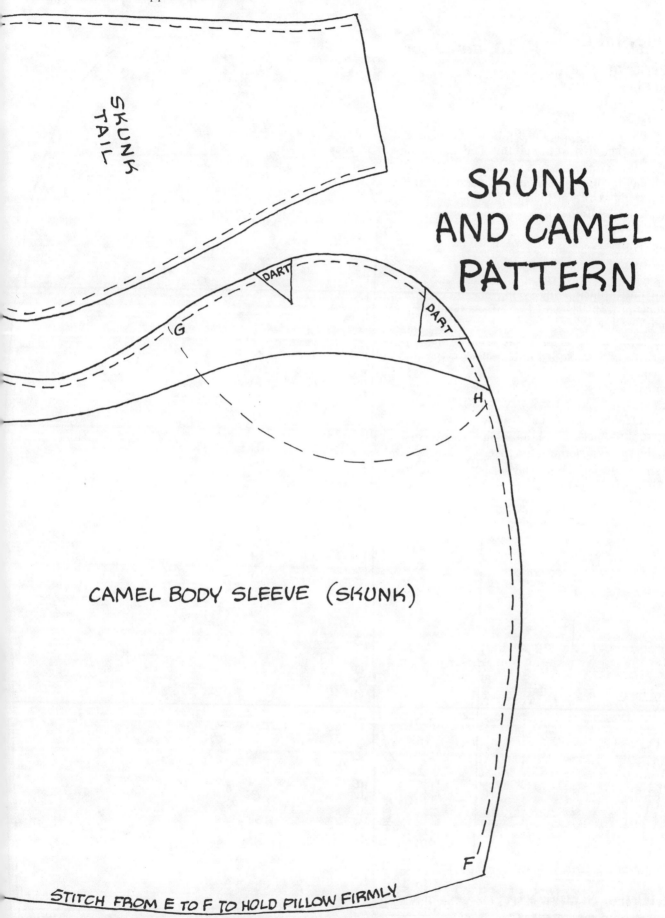

SKUNK
TAIL

SKUNK
AND CAMEL
PATTERN

DART

DART

G

H

CAMEL BODY SLEEVE (SKUNK)

F

STITCH FROM E TO F TO HOLD PILLOW FIRMLY

Optional Sleeves 1A, 1B, and 2 for Patterns on Pages 58-67

by Joan King

Sleeve 1A

1. Place the material on the fold and make it the length from the wrist to the elbow. The size of this pattern will vary.
2. After making the puppet head, cut the dotted short side of the pattern to fit the puppet's neck.
3. Sew along the dotted line.
4. Attach to the head.

Sleeve 1B

1. Cut four of this pattern.
2. Sew front to back along seam lines and reverse.
3. Attach the front sleeve CD to the side of sleeve 1A along the line CD.
4. Note: (This is to be optional arms if they are desired. This is to be added to Number 1A if option is desired.)

Sleeve 2

1. Cut one front on the fold and cut two back halves.
2. Sew front to backs along the seam lines. Reverse.
3. Sew the backs together along AC.
4. Attach to the head, placing the head inside the sleeve to stitch it.

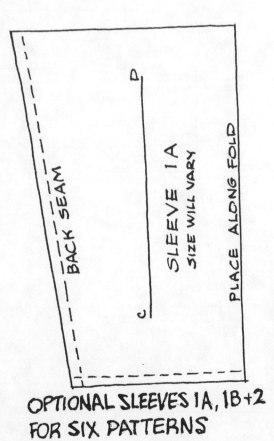

OPTIONAL SLEEVES 1A, 1B + 2
FOR SIX PATTERNS

BACK SEAM

SLEEVE 1A
SIZE WILL VARY

PLACE ALONG FOLD

CUT FOR SLEEVE 2

MAKE NECK LARGER OR SMALLER HERE

CUT FROM SLEEVE 1B

SLEEVES 1B AND 2

Personal Pattern Notes

Chapter 7
MARIONETTES

Marionette Pattern
by Joy Robertson

Shoe and Leg

Cut four patterns of the shoe. Take two patterns and place right sides together and sew around the shoe leaving the dotted lines open. Turn the right sides of the material out. Do the same for the other two pattern pieces.

Cut four innersole patterns from light poster board. Place two innersoles in each shoe.

Assemble the shoe by stuffing the toe of the shoe and continue around to the left and right sides of the shoe. In the center of the shoe place three pennies (for weights). With a needle and thread make a gathering stitch along the dotted lines. Draw the thread until the material is gathered in the center. Wrap the thread around the gathered material three times and tie off the thread. The shoes are ready to attach to the legs.

Cut two of top leg pattern, one for the right side and one for the left side. Remember to cut the material on the fold. Turn the material so the right sides are together. Sew sides A and B with a 2/8-inch seam. At side C turn up a 2/8-inch hem but leave side C open. Turn and stuff.

Cut two of lower leg pattern also. Turn the material so right sides are together. Sew side E with a 2/8-inch seam. At sides D and F turn up a 2/8-inch hem but leave sides D and F open. Turn and stuff.

To connect the leg, take point C and slip it inside point D about 2/8-inch. Sew across these points and this will joint the leg together.

To connect the leg and shoe, take the shoe at point F and insert the gathered material and sew back and forth to attach the shoe to the leg. Take points G and H and stitch behind the leg. At point F catch a few stitches to the top of the shoe to hold it in a right angle position to the leg.

Arm

Cut two of top arm pattern. Turn right sides together. Sew side B with a 2/8-inch seam. At sides A and C, turn up a 2/8-inch seam but leave them open. At side A on the dotted line run a gathering thread and gather. Turn and stuff.

Cut two of lower arm pattern. Turn the right sides together and sew side E. At points D and F turn up a 2/8-inch hem and leave open.

To assemble the arm, take point C and slip it inside point D about 2/8-inch. Sew across these points and this will joint the arm together. Attach the arm at point A to the side of top of body piece. Attach so arm and shoulder will be even.

Hand

Cut four of this pattern. Take two pieces and place the right sides together and sew all sides except the dotted line area. Turn with a sharp-ended object. Place a piece of pipe cleaner the length of each finger and complete the hand by stuffing.

To connect the arm and the hand take the lower arm at point F, insert the open end of the hand until the hand fits against the arm. Sew across to joint the arm and the hand.

Body

Cut two of top of body pattern and turn the right sides of the material together. Sew all sides except the dotted line area. Turn and stuff.

Follow the same instructions for the lower body.

To Connect the Top Body and Lower Body attach the top body and the lower body with a few loops of thread at points A on the top body and points B on the lower body.

Head

Take a Styrofoam ball about four inches in diameter and mark off the eye sockets. Place the thumbs on these markings and press to form the eye sockets. If the ball seems to be a little large for the body, continue to press the styrofoam to the desired size. To add color to the head, take a few drops of liquid make-up, glue, and water and mix them together. Paint the ball with this combination and allow it to dry. At the base of the head, cut a hole about 2 inches deep and ½-inch wide.

To connect the head and body, begin with a dowel pin about ¼-inch wide and about 5 inches long. Drill two holes about an inch apart, measuring from one end of the pin. Allow the drilled holes to go down the back of the top body about an inch from the end of the top body section. Using a needle and a thread, sew through the holes in the dowel attaching it to the material. At the top of the dowel use a ½-inch eye screw. Using a long piece of yarn and a large needle, run it down the top of the head to the neck and loop it through the eye screw and back up through the head again. Use a button to tie off on top of the head. Hair will cover the button.

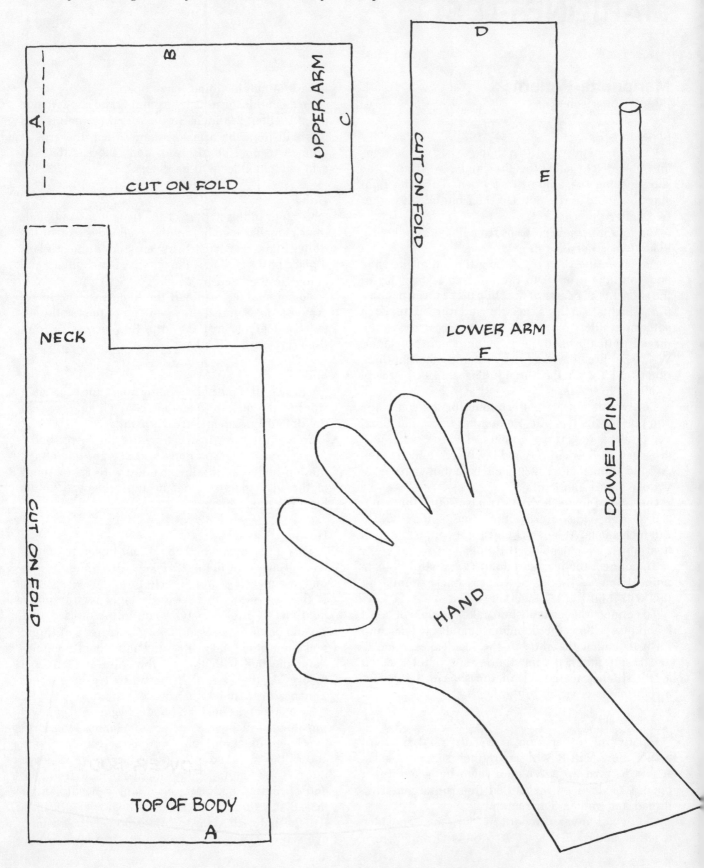

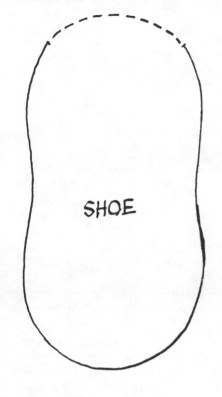

SHOE

MARIONETTE
PATTERN

INNERSOLE

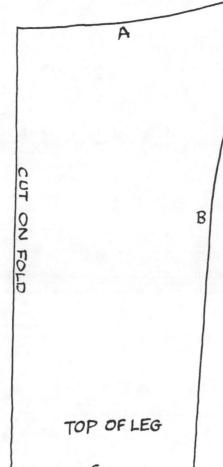

CUT ON FOLD

A

B

C

TOP OF LEG

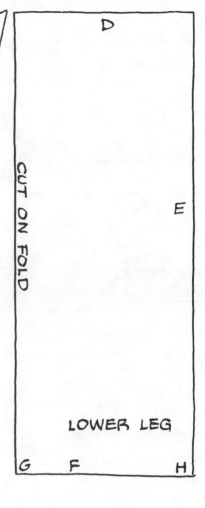

D

CUT ON FOLD

E

LOWER LEG

G F H

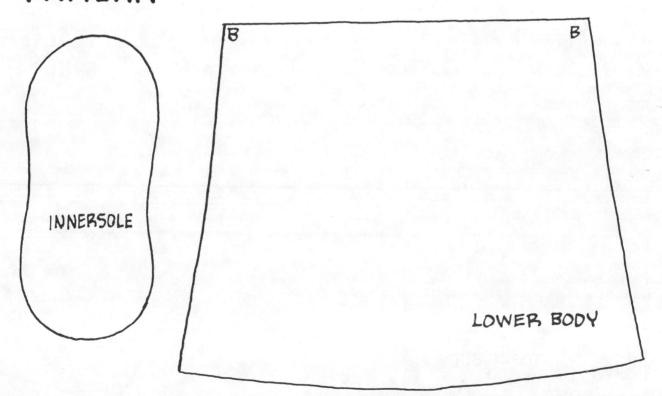

B

B

LOWER BODY

Clothes for the Marionette
by Joy Robertson

Blouse

1. Cut two of this pattern. Remember to cut the pattern on the fold.
2. In the neck area, fold points C down to points D to form a ½-inch casing. Stitch around the casing. In the back of the casing cut a small slit to allow a tie to be sent through and brought back out to make a tie.
3. From points E to F turn up a ¼-inch hem.

Sleeve addition

1. Cut two of this pattern, one for the left and one for the right. Remember to cut on the fold.
2. Attach points A to B.

Tie for the Casing

1. Cut 1 of this pattern. Remember to cut on the fold.
2. Fold the material on the dotted lines and stitch. Run the finished tie through the casing at the neck of the blouse.

Skirt

1. Cut two of this pattern and remember to cut the material on the fold.
2. Along the dotted line, run a gathering stitch. Tie one end of the seam and gather from the other end of the seam. When both pieces of the material have been gathered to fit the waist of the marionette, turn right sides together and sew down both sides. *Note:* always leave the waist large enough for the marionette to step into the skirt without an additional opening in the waistband.
3. Skirt must be hemmed to the desired length. *Note:* Always allow the skirt to come just above the shoes.

Waistband (for skirt)

1. Cut one of this pattern and remember to cut it on the fold.
2. Place the right side of the waistband to the right side of the gathered skirt band. Sew them together just below the gathered stitch. Stitch the waistband down on the inside of the skirt (by hand).

Strap for Shoulders (attached to the skirt)

1. Cut two of this pattern. Remember to cut the material on the fold.
2. Fold the strap and stitch on the dotted lines.

Pocket for the Skirt

1. Cut one of this pattern.
2. Turn the pocket under along the dotted lines and topstitch around the pocket. If the pocket is to be left open, do not sew from points A to B.
3. Attach to the skirt (anywhere).

Neck Ruffle

1. Cut one of this pattern. Remember to cut it on the fold. Turn and sew down the ends. Turn right.
2. Along the dotted line, stitch a gathering seam. Tie one end of the seam and gather from the other end of the seam.
3. Gather the ruffle to fit the neck of the marionette and stitch the ends of the ruffle together (after it is on the marionette).

Hat

1. Cut one of this pattern.
2. Along the dotted lines, attach a light trimming such as lace (with pins).
3. Along the same dotted lines, run a gathering stitch. Tie one end of the seam and gather from the other end of the seam to fit the head of the marionette. When the material has been gathered to fit the head, stitch the hat at this point. Elastic may be used in place of the gathering seam if one finds it easier to assemble.
4. Accessories may be added to the hat. A nob in the top of the hat would be an idea.

Pantaloons (under the skirt)

1. Cut two of this pattern. *Note:* Cut only point A to point B on the fold. Sew right sides together.
2. Fold points A down to points B to form a ¼-inch casing. Stitch around the casing. In the back of the casing cut a small slit to allow a piece of elastic to be run through. Stitch the elastic together and then close the slit in the casing by hand.
3. Take a ¼-inch hem in the pantaloons and lace may be added at the hem also.

Shoe

1. Take the sole of the marionette's shoe and trace it on black felt (any color). Cut out the pattern and glue the felt to the sole of the shoe.
2. Take small pieces of felt and form the sides of the marionette's shoes. Straps may be added. Glue the pieces of felt to the sides of the shoes. Any type of accessory may be added to make the shoe fancier. Adding beads would be an idea.
3. Tempera paint may also be used to color the sole and the shoe. Any color may be used to match the clothing of the marionette.

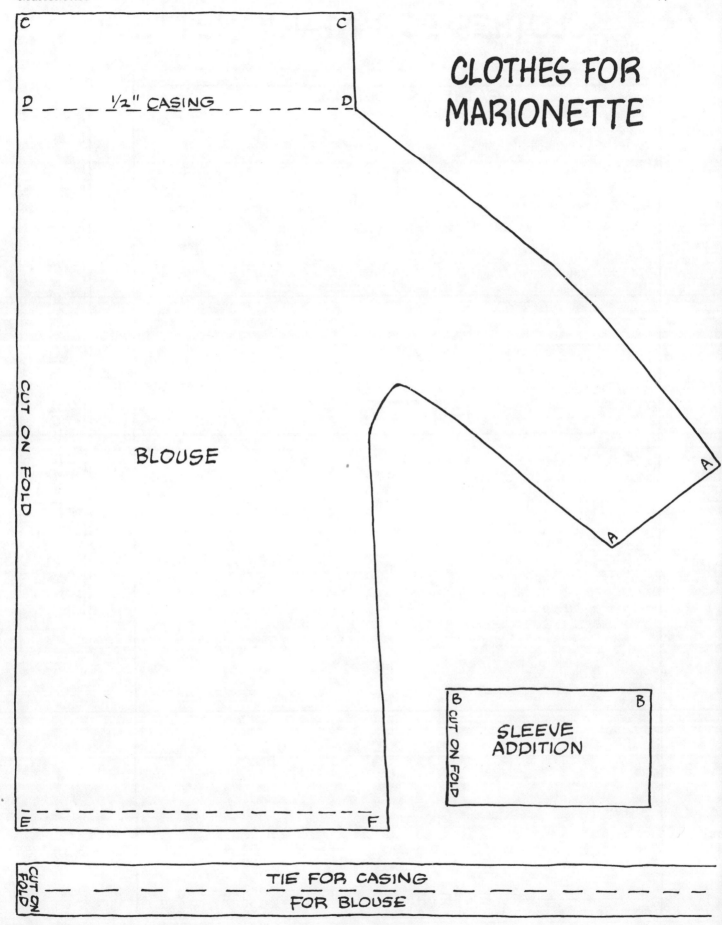

CLOTHES FOR MARIONETTE

C   C

D _ _ _ _ 1/2" CASING _ _ _ _ D

CUT ON FOLD

BLOUSE

A

A

E _ _ _ _ _ _ _ _ F

B CUT ON FOLD

SLEEVE ADDITION

B

CUT ON FOLD

TIE FOR CASING
FOR BLOUSE

CLOTHES FOR MARIONETTE

GATHERING SEAM LINE

CUT ON FOLD

SKIRT

EXTEND TO 13"

STRAP FOR SHOULDERS

CUT ON FOLD

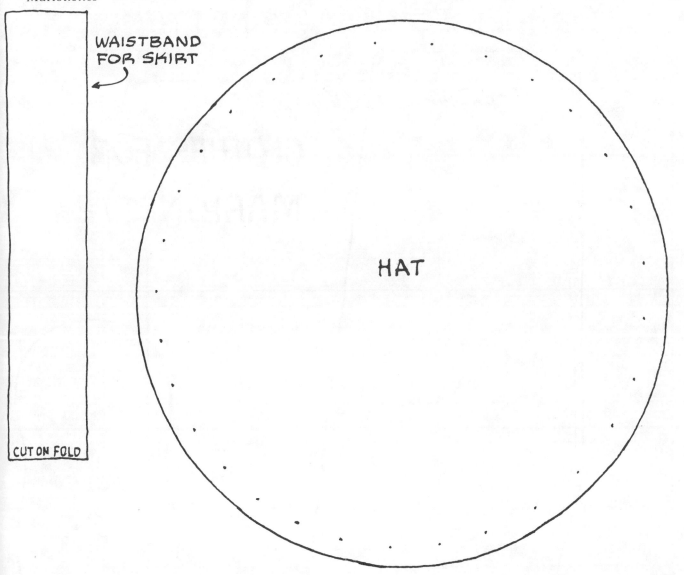

WAISTBAND
FOR SKIRT

CUT ON FOLD

HAT

CLOTHES FOR MARIONETTE

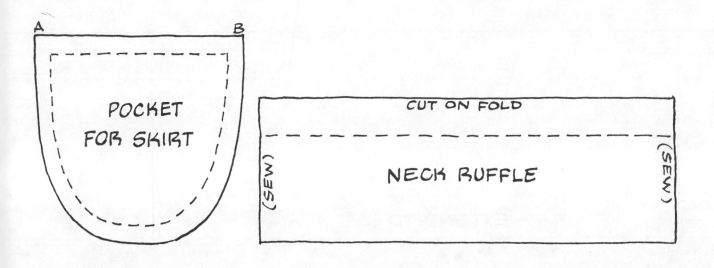

POCKET
FOR SKIRT

CUT ON FOLD

(SEW)

NECK RUFFLE

(SEW)

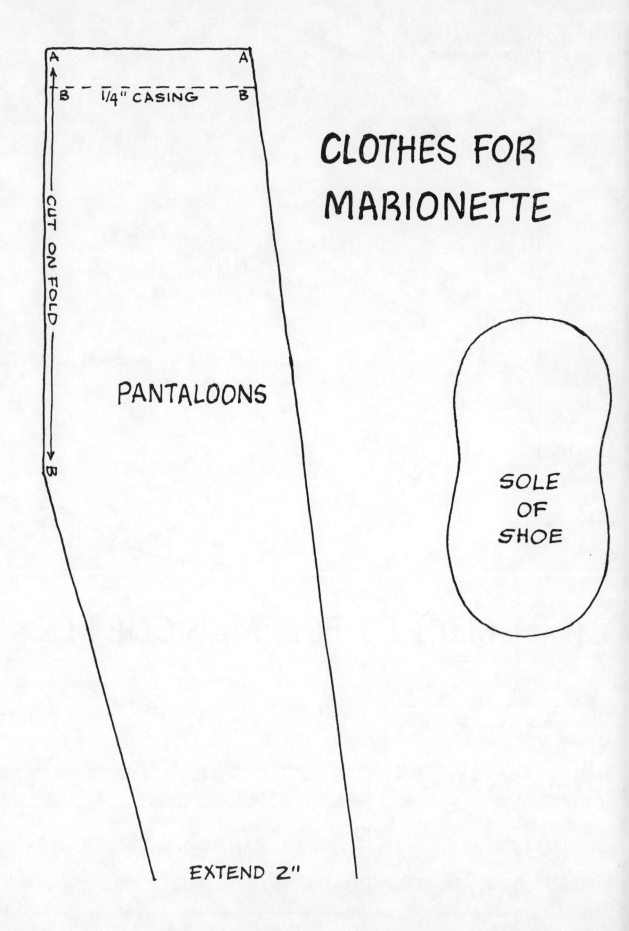

A A

B ¼" CASING B

CUT ON FOLD

CLOTHES FOR MARIONETTE

PANTALOONS

B

SOLE OF SHOE

EXTEND 2"

Wire Marionette
by Doris Goodrich Jones

The wire marionette is constructed similarly to other marionettes. The basic difference is that a wire rod extends from the puppet to the puppeteer. This rod permits greater stability in manipulating the puppet.

Materials Needed: a marionette, wire rod (recommend coat hanger), 4-inch wood strip, spool, and black thread.

1. Run wire through head of marionette and attach securely to body. Length of wire may vary.
2. At top of wire, bend 2 or 3 inches of wire forward.
3. Place 4-inch wood strip glued to a spool on the wire. Curl end of wire.
4. Connect thread from knees of marionette to wood strip. Connect thread from hands to the curl at the end of the wire.

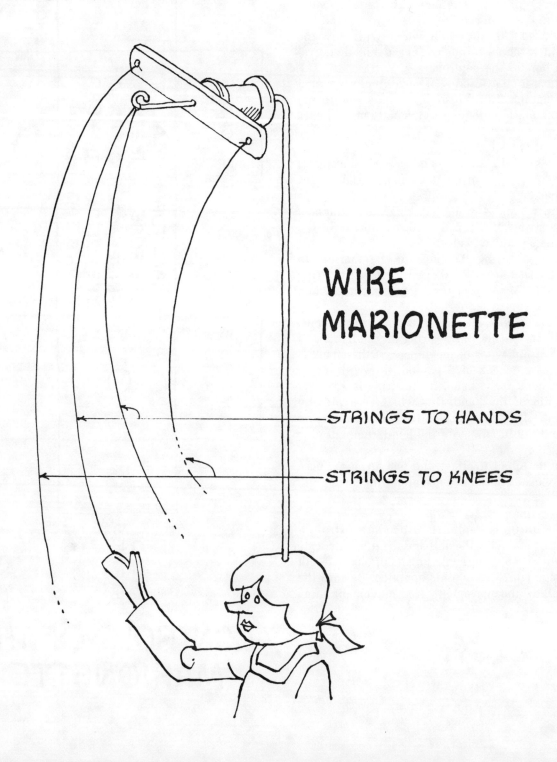

WIRE MARIONETTE

STRINGS TO HANDS

STRINGS TO KNEES

Controls for the Marionette
by Joy Robertson

Controls

1. Using the exact pattern, cut three pieces of wood to fit hand. Attach the cross bar 2¾ inches from one end of the longest piece of wood. Attach the wood by using a U-brad.

2. Measure 1⅜ inches in front of the cross bar (on the longest piece of wood). Attach a ¼-inch dowel pin (about 1 inch long). Attach with a U-brad also. *Note:* Dowel pin may be attached by glue.

3. Measure the center of the piece of wood that has not been used. Cut out a hole which will allow the dowel pin to come through. This is called the removable bar for the controls.

4. Place a ¼-inch eye screw at each number located on the diagram. Run thread from the screw to the joint of the marionette (to provide body movement).

Stringing of the Marionette

1. At points 1 and 2, string the head. Place the strings about the center point on the left and right sides of the head.

2. At points 3 and 4, shoulder strings are attached. Place the strings down a little on the back (in the area of the shoulder blades).

3. At point 5, string the back of the marionette (usually the seat area). Remember to place the string in the center of the seat for a good balance when using this string.

4. At points 6 and 7, attach the strings for the hands. Different placements of the string on the hand will indicate certain types of movement. If the string is attached at the back of the hand, this will give a flat movement to the hand. If the string is attached in the palm of the hand, this will give a pick-up movement. If the string is attached between the thumb and the forefinger of the hand, this will give a natural movement.

5. At points 8 and 9, attach the feet strings. These strings are usually attached just above the knee joint.

A Helpful Hint

It seems to be easier for two people to string a marionette (one holds the doll and the other strings). The length of the strings will depend upon the depth of the stage which the doll is operated. Be sure the strings allow the marionette free movement (long enough).

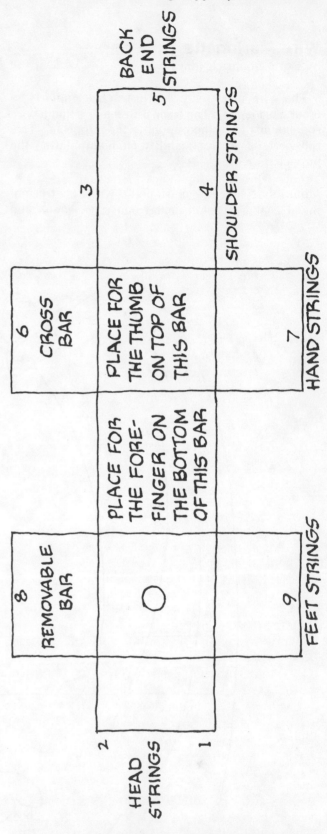

CONTROLS OF THE MARIONETTE

Operating the Marionette
by Joy Robertson

Typical Marionettes
1. Most marionettes have nine strings.
2. Special strings may be added such as a hoop skirt string. Strings may also be deleted such as the feet strings (for dolls with long flowing costumes), the shoulder strings, or the back end string.

General Rules to Follow to Prevent Tangles
1. Always pick up the marionette by the controls.
2. When putting down the marionette, always place the controls on the top of the doll. It is best to replace the marionette on a hook so the strings can hang straight.

Hand Placement for the controls
1. The left hand holds the control bar.
2. The forefinger should be placed under the main cross bar (a little to the front of the bar).
3. Place the thumb on top of the cross bar.
4. Use the little finger of the left hand to create pressure on the shoulder strings.
5. The removable bar is held stationary by the dowel pin and should be operated by the right hand. If you are still not sure of the hand positions, refer to the diagram of the controls.

Tilts of the Bar
1. The bar may be moved to the front and back (back and forth movement).
2. The controls will move from side to side.
3. *Note:* Practice with the marionette to discover the different types of movement one's doll can make.

Walking the Marionette
1. Work the foot bar (removable bar) with the right hand only.
2. The doll will walk easier if given some type of material to walk on such as a rug.
3. Beginning movements should be made slowly.
4. Move one leg forward and allow the other to follow.
5. Remember, practice is the key.

Sitting Procedure
1. Observe people sitting. Notice one's procedure for getting up and going down.
2. The marionette should lean forward when sitting or getting up. Do this slowly.

Movement While Speaking
1. Since the marionette mouth usually does not move when speaking, some type of movement should be made so the audience can tell which doll is speaking.
2. Head and arm movements are good but should not be overdone.

Big Mistakes (in operating the doll)
1. Do not hold the doll too high for walking or standing.
2. Do not hold the doll too low.
3. Be sure the marionette enters the stage and exits the stage on the ground.

Chapter 8
PUPPET STAGES

The primary purpose of a puppet stage is to mask the puppeteer. However, in the process, the stage should enhance the visual qualities of a puppet production. The degree to which this occurs will depend to a great extent on the number of productions over a period of time and funds available.

For the purposes of the puppet ministry there are three categories of stages: makeshift, temporary, and permanent. Makeshift stages may be suitable for classroom Bible story productions. However, if the puppet ministry tours to any extent, or uses technical equipment like lights or sound, a more suitable stage will be necessary. Portable or permanent stages do not need to be extravagant. In fact, if the stage is too colorful, it may distract from the puppets. However, some color is needed to draw attention to the stage.

A good background is crucial to the success of a production. The background determines how well the puppets are visually defined for the audience. A very bright background may be difficult to look at for any extended period of time. Also, it may make it difficult to concentrate on puppets of similar brightness. Bright, warm colors are generally used with the puppets. Therefore, the best backgrounds are darker, solid colors. Deep blues, browns, even black are generally the best for a background. Care must be taken that a puppet is not the same color as the background. In this situation there is obviously a problem in visually picking up the puppet.

The stage should be sturdy although it is not necessary to use heavy materials. One of the most functional and least expensive stages is the PVC pipe stage. These are sturdy, yet they would not support someone sitting on them. It is the puppeteer's responsibility to work with the stage. There is no need for a puppet stage of this nature to support a lot of weight. The only weight directly on the stage should be the curtains. Lights, sound equipment, and other materials should not be supported by this type of stage.

Whatever type of stage is used, be certain curtains or any other masking materials are securely fastened. A puppet production will be brought to an abrupt conclusion if a curtain or structural element collapses.

Shoulder Strap Stage
by Doris Goodrich Jones

Materials Needed: Corrugated cardboard, velvet to cover cardboard, and velvet or other material for straps.

1. Shape the cardboard to desired size according to illustration. Cut holes in cardboard for arms.
2. Cover cardboard with velvet.
3. Attach straps to cardboard and adjust size to fit person.
4. Curtain may be hung in front of velvet covered box if desired.
5. Puppets are manipulated through the holes.

CARDBOARD
SHOULDER STRAP
STAGE

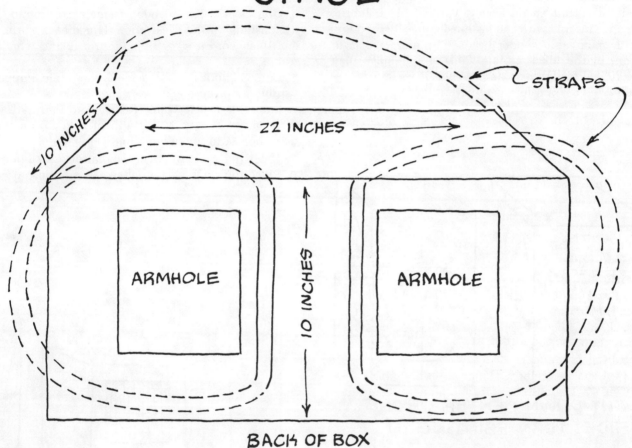

STRAPS

10 INCHES

22 INCHES

ARMHOLE

ARMHOLE

10 INCHES

BACK OF BOX

Refrigerator Box Stage
by Sarah Walton Miller

To build a refrigerator box stage, ask the merchant to remove the bottom and top of the carton and lift it up off the appliance uncut. Then cut it down the center of one side, not the corner. This makes a large screen, with a narrow panel on each end and 3 wider panels between. Turn the inside out to conceal the printing. In the center wide panel, elbow high, cut a window, 2 inches from the top and 2 inches from the fold at the sides. On the inside (printed side) hang a curtain made from 1 yard of black fabric, strung on a fine wire and fastened above the window with removable copper brads. The puppet acts in front of the black curtain. This simple stage may be folded to carry or store. When it wears out, remove the curtain to a new carton.

Bible Puppet Stage
by Doris Goodrich Jones

Materials Needed: ¼- or ⅛-inch plywood, hinges, 1-by-1 or 1-by-2-inch lumber for curtain frame, corduroy or other fabric for the frame, fabric for front curtain, and wire hooks.

1. Cut two pieces of plywood. Each piece should be 12 inches wide and 60 inches long.
2. Hinge the plywood pieces together so they fold easily.
3. Construct a light wooden frame according to the dimensions on the illustration. Hinge each corner.
4. Attach corduroy or other fabric to the wooden frame.
5. Connect hooks to the inside of the frame. Puppets can hang on the hooks.
6. Staple or tack a 60-inch curtain to the platform to form the apron. The length of the curtain may vary, but 24 to 30 inches should be plenty.
7. If desired, paint or cover the platform with fabric.
8. Place the stage on two chairs or a table.

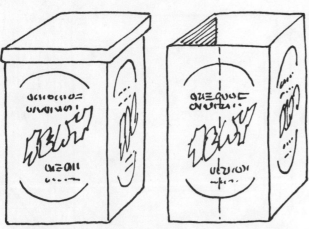

CUT DOWN CENTER OF ONE SIDE. TURN PRINTING IN

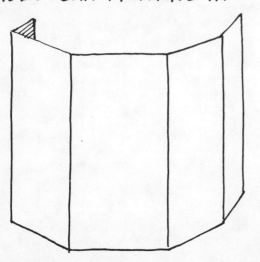

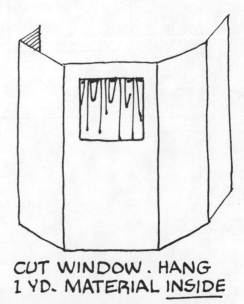

CUT WINDOW. HANG 1 YD. MATERIAL <u>INSIDE</u>

REFRIGERATOR BOX STAGE

POSITION OF PUPPETEER

AUDIENCE

BIBLE PUPPET STAGE

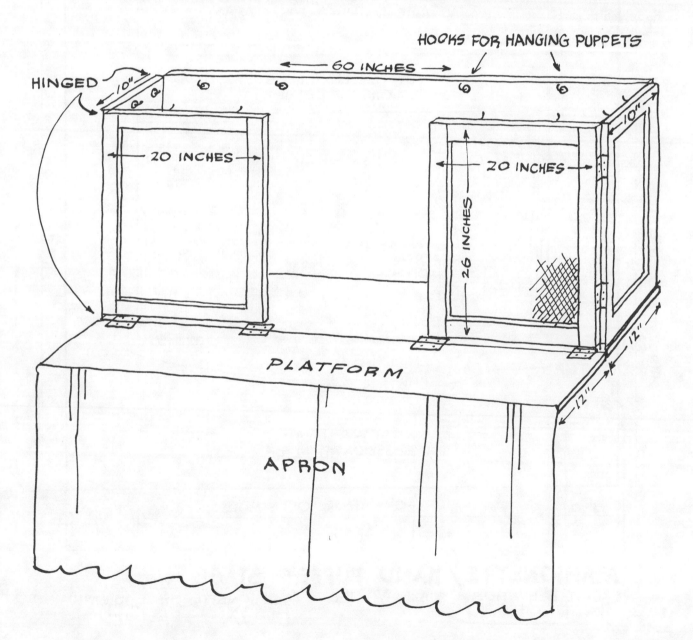

HOOKS FOR HANGING PUPPETS

HINGED

10"

60 INCHES

20 INCHES

20 INCHES

26 INCHES

10"

12"

12"

PLATFORM

APRON

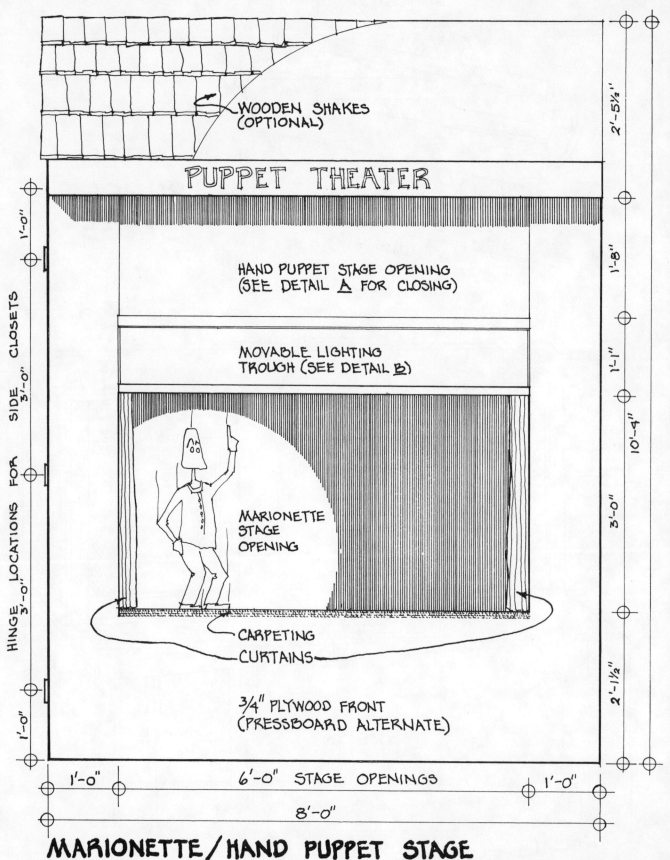

MARIONETTE / HAND PUPPET STAGE
FRONT ELEVATION   SCALE: ¾" = 1'-0"   (MARIONETTE STAGE SHOWN)

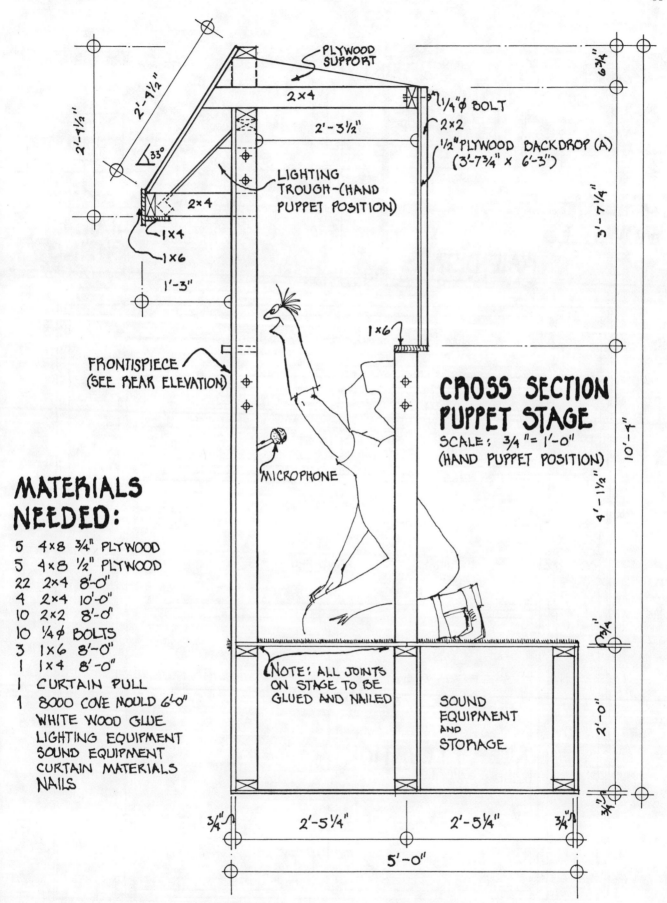

PLYWOOD SUPPORT

2×4

2'-4½"

2'-4½"

2'-4½"

35°

2×4

1×4

1×6

1'-3"

LIGHTING TROUGH–(HAND PUPPET POSITION)

2'-3½"

¼"∅ BOLT

2×2

½" PLYWOOD BACKDROP (A)
(3'-7¾" × 6'-3")

6¾"

3'-7¼"

1×6

FRONTISPIECE
(SEE REAR ELEVATION)

MICROPHONE

CROSS SECTION PUPPET STAGE
SCALE: ¾" = 1'-0"
(HAND PUPPET POSITION)

10'-1"

4'-1½"

¾"

MATERIALS NEEDED:

5 4×8 ¾" PLYWOOD
5 4×8 ½" PLYWOOD
22 2×4 8'-0"
4 2×4 10'-0"
10 2×2 8'-0"
10 ¼∅ BOLTS
3 1×6 8'-0"
1 1×4 8'-0"
1 CURTAIN PULL
1 8000 CONE MOULD 6'-0"
WHITE WOOD GLUE
LIGHTING EQUIPMENT
SOUND EQUIPMENT
CURTAIN MATERIALS
NAILS

NOTE: ALL JOINTS ON STAGE TO BE GLUED AND NAILED

SOUND EQUIPMENT AND STORAGE

2'-0"

¾"

3'-4"

2'-5¼"

2'-5¼"

5'-0"

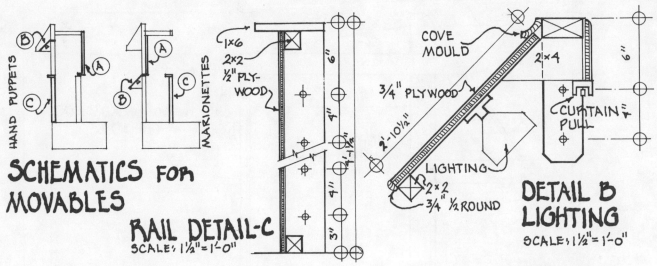

SCHEMATICS FOR MOVABLES

RAIL DETAIL-C
SCALE: 1½"=1'-0"

DETAIL B LIGHTING
SCALE: 1½"=1'-0"

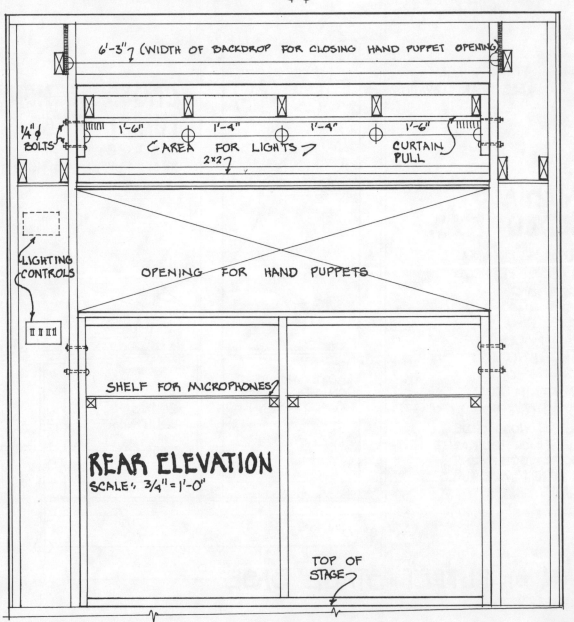

REAR ELEVATION
SCALE: 3/4"=1'-0"

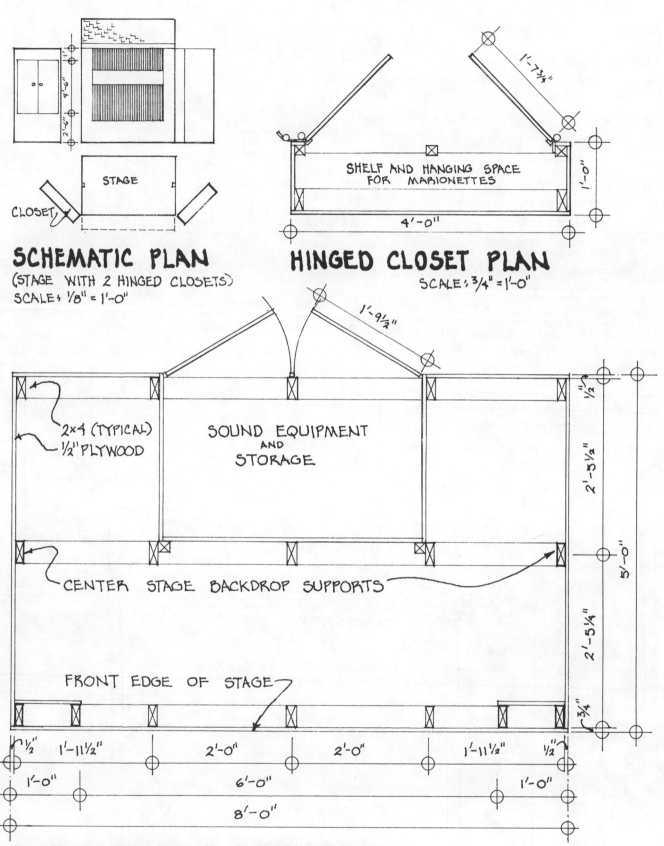

SCHEMATIC PLAN
(STAGE WITH 2 HINGED CLOSETS)
SCALE: 1/8" = 1'-0"

STAGE

CLOSET

HINGED CLOSET PLAN
SCALE: 3/4" = 1'-0"

SHELF AND HANGING SPACE
FOR MARIONETTES

1'-7¾"

1'-0"

4'-0"

1'-9½"

2×4 (TYPICAL)
½" PLYWOOD

SOUND EQUIPMENT
AND
STORAGE

CENTER STAGE BACKDROP SUPPORTS

FRONT EDGE OF STAGE

½"
2'-5½"
5'-0"
2'-5¼"
¾"

½"   1'-11½"   2'-0"   2'-0"   1'-11½"   ½"

1'-0"   6'-0"   1'-0"

8'-0"

PLAN of PUPPET STAGE BASE
SCALE: 3/4" = 1'-0"

Plastic Pipe Stage*

Materials Needed:

    4 — 4-inch square woodblocks (stands)
    4 — flanges (cast iron)
    4 — plastic connectors (for stands)
    1 — 1½ inch PVC pipe
    2 — 90-degree PVC connectors
    2 — 45-degree PVC connectors
    2 — 4-inch pieces of PVC pipe
    1 — 10-foot PVC pipe
    2 — 3½-foot PVC pipe
    4 — 4-foot PVC pipe
    2 — "T" PVC pipe connectors

1. Construct according to illustration.
2. Cover pipe stage with curtains (recommend dark velvet).
3. An additional backdrop may be constructed. It should be 7 to 8 feet high, about as long as the stage, and stand independently. It can also be covered with a dark velvet.

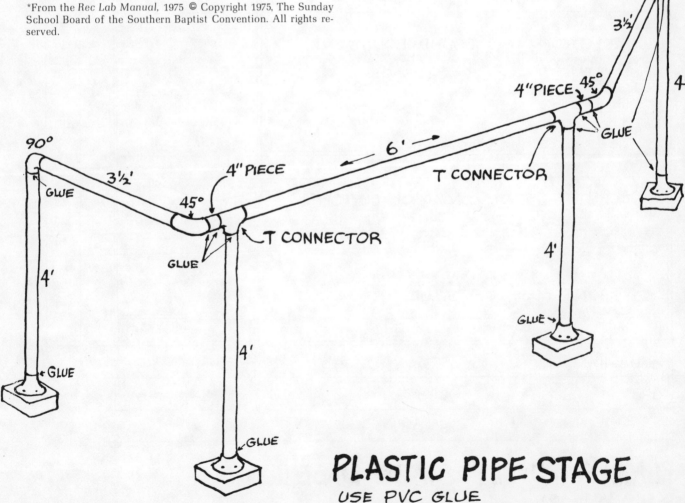

PLASTIC PIPE STAGE
USE PVC GLUE

APPENDIX A
LIGHTING COMPANIES*
(rental and/or sales)

American Scenic Company
11 Andrews
Greenville, South Carolina, 29602

American Stage Lighting Co.
1331c North Avenue
New Rochelle, New York 10804

Arizona Theatre Equipment
1410 East Washington
Phoenix, Arizona 85036

Associated Theatrical Contractors
307 West Eightieth
Kansas City, Missouri 64114

Atlanta Costume Company
2409 Piedmont Road, N.E.
Atlanta, Georgia 30324

Bash Stage Lighting Company
715 Grand Street
Hoboken, New Jersey 07030

Brite Lites
1196 West Third Avenue
Columbus, Ohio 43212

Capitol Stage Equipment Company
3121 North Penn
Oklahoma City, Oklahoma 73112

Capron Lighting Company, Inc.
278 West Street
Boston, Massachusetts 02194

Central Control Company
Box 16
Downers Grove, Illinois 60515

Decor Davis Electronics Corp.
4711 East Fifth Street
Austin, Texas 78702

Electro Controls
2975 South Second, West
Salt Lake City, Utah 84115

Electronics Diversified, Inc.
0625 Southwest Florida Street
Portland, Oregon 97219

Grand Stage Lighting Company
630 West Lake Street
Chicago, Illinois 60606

Hodges Theatre Supply Company
2927 Jackson Avenue
New Orleans, Louisiana 70125

Houston Scenic Studios
7026 Sherman
Houston, Texas 77011

Hub Electric Company
904 Industrial Drive
Elmhurst, Illinois 60126

Jack A. Frost
234 Piquette Avenue
Detroit, Michigan 48202

Kentucky Scenic Studios
6405 Mayfair Avenue
Prospect, Kentucky 40059

Kliegl Brothers, Inc.
32-32 Forty-Eighth Avenue
Long Island City, New York 11101
or
2333 North Street
Burbank, California 95104

Lehigh Electric Products Company
3317 Lehigh Street
Allentown, Pennsylvania 18103

Lighting by Lane
4304 Randel Drive
Wichita Falls, Texas 76309

Little Stage Lighting Company
10507 Harry Hines Boulevard
Box 20211
Dallas, Texas 20211

L & M Stagecraft Company
1740 East Seventeenth Street
Cleveland, Ohio 44114

Los Angeles Stage Lighting
1451 Venice Boulevard
Los Angeles, California 90006

Mosetrol Theater Technology
230 Kamena Street
Fairview, New Jersey 07022

National Stage Lighting
925 Tenth Street, N.W.
Washington, D.C. 20001

Northwestern Costume House
3203 North Highway #100
Minneapolis, Minnesota 55422

Olesen Company
1535 Ivar Avenue
Hollywood, California 90028

Paramount Theatrical Supplies
32 West Twentieth Street
New York, New York 10011

Spradlin Brothers Stage Lighting
5700 Mallory Road
Red Oak, Georgia 30272

Stagecraft Industries
8 Dellwood Road
White Plains, New York 10605
or
1302 Northwest Kearney Street
Portland, Oregon 97208
or
10237 Main Street
Bellevue, Washington 98004

Stage Engineering & Supply Co.
Box 2002
Colorado Springs, Colorado 80901

Stage Equipment & Lighting
12231 Northeast 13 Court
North Miami, Florida 33161

Stage Lighting Rental Service
170 Gilbert Avenue
New Haven, Connecticut 06511

Standard Theatre Supply Company
125 Higgins Street
Greensboro, North Carolina 27406

Superior Electric Company
383 Middle Street
Bristol, Connecticut 06010

Texas Scenic Company
5423 Jackwood Drive
San Antonio, Texas 78228

Theatre Production Service
59 Fourth Avenue
New York, New York 10036

Theatrical Scenic & Prop Studio
320 West Forty-Eighth Street
New York, New York 10036

Tidewater Lighting
3580 North Ingleside Drive
Norfolk, Virginia 23502

Times Square Stage Lighting Company
318 West Forty-Seventh Street
New York, New York 10036

Tobins Lake Studios
2650 7-Mile Road
South Lyon, Michigan 48178

Tri-Stage Theatre Supply
151 Vance
Memphis, Tennessee 38103

Ward Leonard Electric Company, Inc.
34 South Street
Mount Vernon, New York 10550

APPENDIX B
BIBLIOGRAPHY

Abbe, Dorothy. The Dwiggins Marionettes: *A Complete Experimental Theatre in Miniature*. Boston: Plays, Inc., 1970.

Adair, Margaret W. *Do-It-In-A-Day Puppets: For Beginners*. New York: John Day Co., Inc., 1964.

Alkema, Chester J. *Puppet-Making*. New York: Sterling Publishing Co., 1971.

Anderson, Benny E. *Let's Start a Puppet Theater*. Cincinnati: Van Nos Reinhold, Co., 1973.

Arnott, Peter D. *Plays Without People: Puppetry and Serious Drama*. Bloomington: Indiana University Press, 1964.

Baird, Bil. *Art of the Puppet*. Boston: Plays, Inc., 1966.

Beresford, Margaret. *How to Make Puppets and Teach Puppetry*. New York: Taplinger Publishing Co., Inc., 1966.

Binyon, Helen. *Puppetry Today*. New York: Watson-Guptill Productions, 1966.

Bodor, John J. *Creating and Presenting Hand Puppets*. New York: Reinhold, 1967.

Bramall, Eric and Somerville, Christopher C. *Expert Puppet Technique*. Boston: Plays, Inc. 1966.

Crothers, J. Frances. *Puppeteer's Library Guide: A Bibliographic Index to the Literature of the World Puppet Theatre*. Metuchen, N.J.: Scarecrow Press, Inc., 1971.

Cummings, Richard. *101 Hand Puppets*. New York: David McKay & Co., 1962.

Currell, David. *The Complete Book of Puppetry*. Boston: Plays, Inc., 1975.

Currell, David. *Puppetry for School Children*. Newton, Mass: C. T. Branford Co., 1970.

Dean, Audrey Vincente. *Puppets That Are Different*. New York: Taplinger, 1973.

Dietl, Ulla. *Evas Dolls and Puppets*. New York: Crown Publishing, Inc., 1972.

Engler, Larry and Fijan, Carol. *Making Puppets Come Alive*. New York: Taplinger Publishing Co., Inc., 1973.

Fettig, Hansjuergen. *Hand and Rod Puppets*. Boston: Plays, Inc., 1974.

Ficklen, Bessie A. *Handbook of Fist Puppets*. Philadelphia: J. B. Lippincott Co., 1935.

Fraser, Peter. *Introducing Puppetry*. New York: Watson-Guptill Publications, Inc., 1968.

French, Susan. *Presenting Marionettes*. Cincinnati: Van Nos Reinhold, Co., 1964.

Green, M. C. and Targett, B. R. *Space Age Puppets and Masks*. Boston: Plays, Inc., 1969.

Hopper, Grizella H. *Puppet Making Through the Grades*. Worcester, Mass.: Davis Publishing, Inc., 1966.

Howard, Vernon. *Puppet and Pantomime Plays*. New York: Sterling Publishing Co., 1962.

Hutchings, Margaret. *Making and Using Finger Puppets*. New York: Taplinger Publishing Co., Inc., 1973.

Kampmann, Lothar. *Creating with Puppets*. Cincinnati: Van Nos Reinhold, Co., 1972.

Kotowski, Joanne. *Say It with Puppets*. Dayton, Ohio: Pflaum-Standard, 1975.

Lee, Miles. *Puppet Theatre Production and Manipulation*. Fair Lawn, N.J.: Essential Books, 1958.

Lewis, Shari. *Making Easy Puppets*. New York: E. P. Dutton, 1967.

Lewis, Shari and Oppenheimer, Lillian. *Folding Paper Puppets*. New York: Stein and Day, 1962.

London, Carolyn. *You Can Be a Puppeteer*. Chicago: Moody Press, 1972.

MacNamara, Desmond. *Puppets and Puppet-Plays*. New York: Horizon Press, 1966.

McLaren, Esme. *Making Glove Puppets*. Boston: Plays, Inc., 1973.

Moloney, Joan. *Making Puppets & Puppet Theatres*. New York: Frederick Fell, 1974.

Morris, Victoria S. *The Hand Puppet Play-Book*. Oakland, Ca.: V.S. Morris, 1974.

Morton, Brenda. *Needlework Puppets*. Boston: Plays, Inc., 1964.

Mulholland, John. *Practical Puppetry*. New York: Arco Publishing Co., Inc., 1961.

Niculescu, Margaret, ed. *Puppet Theatre of the Modern World*. Boston: Plays, Inc. 1967.

Philpott, A. R. *Modern Puppetry*. Boston: Plays, Inc. 1967.

———. *Dictionary of Puppetry*. Boston: Plays, Inc., 1969.

Reiniger, Lotte. *Shadow Theatres and Shadow Films*. New York: Watson-Guptill Publications, Inc., 1970.

Renfro, Nancy. *Puppets for Play Production*. New York: Funk and Wagnalls, 1969.

Reynolds, Joyce. *Puppet Shows That Reach and Teach Children*. Springfield, Mo.: Gospel Publishing House, 1972.

Richter, Dorothy. *Puppets and Puppet Plays*. New York: Frederick Fell, 1970.

Robinson, Stuart and Robinson, Patricia. *Exploring*

Puppetry. Taplinger Publishing Co., Inc., 1967.

Ross, Laura. *Finger Puppets: Easy to Make and Fun to Use.* New York: Lothrop, Lee and Shepard, Co., 1971.

_____. *Hand Puppets: How to Make and Use Them.* New York: Lothrop, Lee and Shapard Co., 1969.

_____. *Holiday Puppets and Plays.* New York: Lee & Shepard, Co., 1974.

Rutter, Vicki. *A B C Puppetry.* Boston: Plays, Inc., 1969.

Snook, Barbara. *Puppets.* Newton Center, Mass.: Charles T. Branford Co., 1966.

Still, William F. *Charming Children with Puppets.* Boston: Branden Press, Inc., 1969.

Tichenor, Tom. *Tom Tichenor's Puppets.* Nashville: Abingdon Press, 1971.

Williams, DeAtna M. *More Paper-Bag Puppets.* Belmont, Ca.: Featon Publishing Co., 1968.

Worrell, Estelle Ansley. *Be a Puppeteer.* New York: McGraw-Hill, 1969.